Z701 .K94 1983
Kyle, Hedi
Library materials
preservation manual :
practical methods for

.K94
1983

4184

Z701 .K94 1983
Kyle, Hedi
Library materials
preservation manual :
practical methods for

LIBRARY MATERIALS
PRESERVATION MANUAL

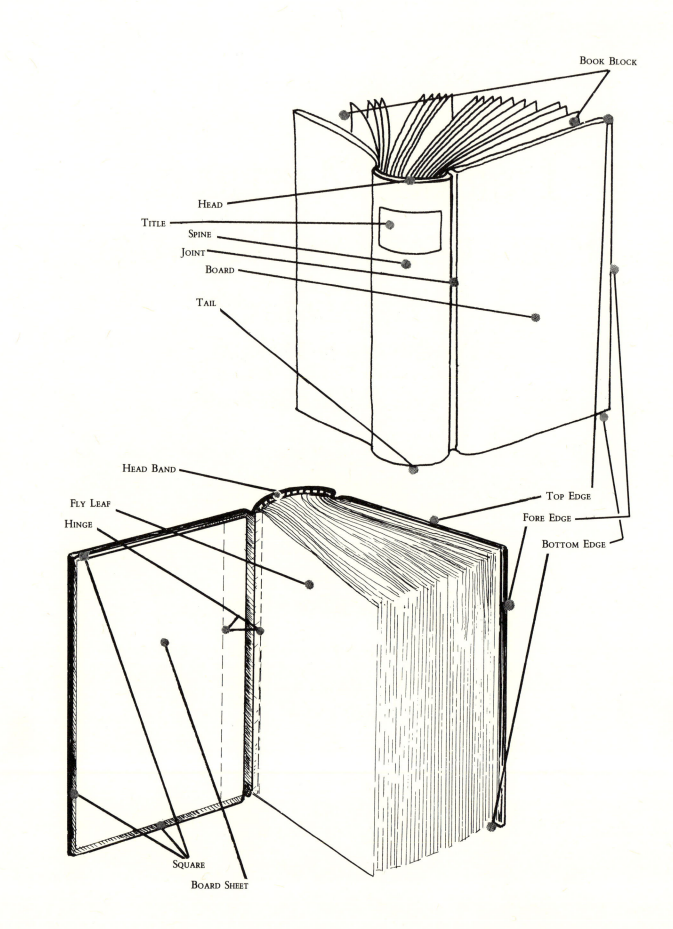

BOOK BLOCK

HEAD

TITLE

SPINE

JOINT

BOARD

TAIL

HEAD BAND

FLY LEAF

HINGE

TOP EDGE

FORE EDGE

BOTTOM EDGE

SQUARE

BOARD SHEET

Library Materials Preservation Manual

Practical Methods
for Preserving Books, Pamphlets
and Other Printed Materials

■

HEDI KYLE
With Contributions By
Nelly Balloffet
Judith Reed
Virginia Wisniewski-Klett

■

Illustrated By
HEDI KYLE

NICHOLAS T. SMITH
Publisher
Bronxville, New York

CAUTION

Properly handled, all of the materials mentioned in this manual are safe for books and humans so far as has been determined. Because there are many levels of toxicity, some chemicals may be used with relative safety in a well-ventilated room or outdoors, while others will require a face mask and fume hood to help avoid inhalation or skin contact. The fact that some chemicals can be absorbed through skin contact should not be dismissed lightly. If a particular product such as a solvent or spray is being considered for use, first ascertain whether the chemicals that it contains are safe for use and under what conditions. Information on toxicity can be obtained by contacting *Art Hazards Information Center*, 5 Beekman Street, New York, New York 10038, (212) 227-6220.

The authors and publisher take no responsibility for any harm which may be caused by the use or misuse of the information contained in this book, or by the use or misuse of any materials or processes mentioned in the book.

Copyright © 1983 by THE NEW YORK BOTANICAL GARDEN

All rights reserved. No part of this publication may be reproduced or used in any form or by any means—graphic, electronic or mechanical—without prior written permission of the publisher.

NICHOLAS T. SMITH
Box 66
Bronxville, New York 10708

Library of Congress Cataloging in Publication Data

Kyle, Hedi.
    Library materials preservation manual.

    Bibliography: p.
    Includes index.
    1. Books—Conservation and restoration—Handbooks, manuals, etc. 2. Paper—Preservation—Handbooks, manuals, etc. 3. Library materials—Conservation and restoration—Handbooks, manuals, etc. I. Title.
Z701.K94 1983   025.8'4   83-578
ISBN 0-935164-10-3

Printed in the United States of America

LMPM | TABLE OF CONTENTS

RAMSEY LIBRARY
UNC-Asheville
Asheville, NC

In an effort to encourage the formation and development of library materials preservation programs, the New York Botanical Garden Book Preservation Center, through a grant from the H.W. Wilson Foundation, continued by the National Endowment for the Humanities and H.W. Wilson, has carried out extensive research toward the development of a program for teaching preservation techniques to library personnel. This training program has previously been made available only through workshops and the worksheets that form the basis for this manual. The methods included have been carefully tested for simplicity, safety and soundness.

Through research and feedback gleaned from Book Preservation Center workshops, many of the commonly encountered problems related to the preservation of library materials have been identified. Basic treatments for many of these problems and, in some cases options, have been defined and written up for this manual. Because many of the problems do not necessarily pertain *only* to rare or highly important materials, simplified methods have been developed, while other methods have been revised, in order to increase their economic feasibility.

The considerations of safety and soundness are very important. Safety, as it relates to the worker using preservation tools *and* to the library materials being preserved. Soundness, as it relates to the methods used *and* to the preserved state of the materials after all work is completed.

The information provided is not intended to cover all aspects of preservation treatment. The methods and techniques that are discussed in this manual can be used as permanent or temporary "hold for professional treatment" remedies. Because the techniques described are considered *reversible*, they can be temporary or permanent and should be used with this factor in mind. Reversibility is a benefit that also provides a degree of security when working with rare or highly important materials. If after reconsideration more suitable preservation options are discovered, reversibility makes change possible.

Due to the limited number of preservation training programs, this manual has been geared to the needs of the aspiring preservation librarian or layman. It is intended to be an introduction to the techniques of preservation. Where library materials, particularly those that are rare, are in an *advanced* state of deterioration, there is no substitute for a trained, experienced professional restorer/conservator.

In offering guidance to the user we would suggest a thorough reading of this manual as a prerequisite to use. Many of the methods can be utilized as both primary or secondary (optional) treatments. Understanding the available possibilities will help in defining problems and in choosing the most satisfactory solutions.

The preparation of a manual such as this cannot be done without the counsel, criticism, involvement and generous help of many people from within the field and without. We would like to gratefully acknowledge:

Walter Allweil, Bobbi Angell, Janet Baldwin, Paul Banks, Helga Borck, Ann Botshon, Leonora Cimilucca, Patricia Curtin, Robert De Candido, Jerilyn G. Davis, Cathie Donnelly, Mindell Dubansky, Lucy Espicciato, Deborah Evetts, Doris Freitag, Gary Frost, Suzanne Garrett, Maria Grandinette, Jane Greenfield, Carolyn Horton, Steven Johnson, Dorothy Macdonald, Barbara Mauriello, Ellen McCrady, Sherilyn Ogden, Werner Rebsamen, Nancy Russell, Susan Swartzburg, Catherine Vergara, Gay Walker.

For her continued good council and support, special thanks to Laura S. Young. For their continued interest in and support of this project, special thanks to both John F. Reed, Vice-President, The New York Botanical Garden and Charles R. Long, Assistant Vice-President and Director of the Library, The New York Botanical Garden, Bronx, New York.

Our gratitude goes to both the National Endowment of the Humanities (NEH) and The H.W. Wilson Foundation for their continued support of the Book Preservation Center during the preparation of this manual. We would also like to express our thanks to Nina Martin, Renée Roff and Elaine DiLorenzo for typing the manuscript and to Lee Ann Martin for proofreading at several stages of the project. Our last acknowledgements must go to all those who have attended the Book Preservation Center workshops over the past three years—for the welcome constructive criticism and comments about the methods found in this manual.

Hedi Kyle
Nelly Balloffet
Judith Reed
Virginia Wisniewski-Klett

Book Preservation Center
The New York Botanical Garden
Bronx, New York
1982

To differentiate between materials pictured in each series of illustrations, patterns have been assigned to each type of material. Where two patterns of similar design must be placed side by side, a substitute pattern has been used to designate *one* of the materials in order to facilitate identification and coverage of both materials. To simplify the use of this key, a paper marker should be inserted at this page for easy reference.

  PRESSBOARD

 BRISTOL

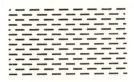 MAP FOLDER STOCK

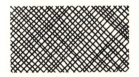 OLD CLOTH COVERING

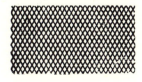 NEW CLOTH COVERING

 ACID FREE WRAPPING PAPER

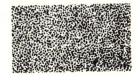 WASTE / SCRAP PAPER

(Continued on the next page)

(Continued from the previous page)

JAPANESE PAPER

WAXED PAPER

POLY-WEB SUPPORT
FOR WET PAPER

ADHESIVE:
PVA AND PASTE,
OR PASTE ONLY

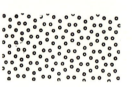

ADHESIVE: PASTE ONLY

ABBREVIATIONS:

    H = Height
    W = Width
    T = Thickness
PVA = polyvinyl acetate (adhesive)

Italicized words are defined elsewhere in this Glossary.

ACID-FREE	This term is loosely used, in the preservation field, for materials which are either pH neutral or alkaline buffered.
ADHESIVE BINDING	A binding method used for securing single sheets along one edge using only an adhesive. A stronger binding results if the *leaves* are in a fanned position when the adhesive is applied. Paperback books are typically, though not always, adhesive bound. Hard-cover books are not usually bound this way. Also referred to as Perfect Binding.
ARCHIVAL	Of sufficiently neutral make-up to be considered safe for long term use in the preservation of library materials.
BACK	See *spine*.
BACKBONE	See *spine*.
BANDS	The covered cords extending across the spine of a book. If the cords are not recessed, they form ridges across the spine of the book known as raised bands. The terms band and *cord* are sometimes used interchangeably.
BINDER'S BOARD	Gray board available in a variety of thicknesses. In appearance, it is similar to the board stock of note pads. Used for the covers of books.
BINDING, n.	The cover of a volume. Also refers to a hard- or finely-bound book.
v.	The process of forming a single unit from single leaves, signatures, or issues of periodicals, or of covering such a unit.
BINDING EDGE	See *spine*.
BLOTTER	Thick, unsized paper. The absence of sizing allows the blotter to be absorbent.
BOARD SHEET	That portion of an *endpaper* which is pasted to the inside of the *board* of a book. Sometimes referred to as a *pastedown*.

BOARD(S)	1. Pressing boards are often referred to simply as boards.
	2. Pliable, fibrous materials such as *binder's board, bristol, pressboard,* or *map folder stock.*
	3. In binding this term refers to the hard covers on the back of the book.
BOND PAPER	A strong, *durable* paper. Also available as *Acid-free Bond.*
BONE FOLDER	A small, hand-held tool made of bone (or plastic), used in folding and other operations.
BOOK BLOCK	The text pages, or "insides" of a book or pamphlet.
BOOK CLOTH	Cotton or linen cloth which has been *sized* with starch, pyroxylin-coated or impregnated. Book cloth possesses characteristics more similar to paper than to cloth. The *grain* of book cloth runs parallel to the *selvage edge.*
BOOKPLATE	A book owner's identification label. Usually pasted to the inside front *pastedown* of a book. Also referred to as *Ex Libris.*
BRISTOL	A heavy weight paper, the surface of which is hard, smooth and, on some types, glazed. File folders are usually made of bristol. Used here to make enclosures and as a pliable board incorporated into other preservation methods.
BUCKRAM	A type of heavy, strong *book cloth.* Available *starch-filled* or *pyroxylin-coated* or *-impregnated.*
BULLDOG CLIPS	Heavy-gauge metal clips. Used to hold pages that are to be side-sewn, to hold a *jig* in place or, used in conjunction with waxed paper and binder's board, to protect materials being worked on.
CALENDERING	The smoothing or glossing of a paper's surface by passing it between metal rollers.

CASE

A case is made up of the boards and spine of a book and can be covered with leather, cloth or paper. The case is made separately and joined to the *book block* near the end of the binding process. Case bindings date back to the 1820's. Trade books (as opposed to special editions) are "case-bound" or "cased." A case does not refer to a box (*clam-shell box*).

CHAIN LINES

See p. 41.

CHEMISE

A protective *wrapper* placed around a book or pamphlet which is then placed in an *enclosure* such as a *slipcase*. A chemise protects the *spine* from light and dust and the *boards* from abrasion during insertion into or removal from an enclosure.

CLAM-SHELL BOX

A protective *enclosure* consisting of a case and two trays, which fit into one another. Used for books, pamphlets, papers and other library materials.

COCKLING

Wrinkling or puckering.

COLLATE

To make certain that all printed paginated and unpaginated portions of a book or pamphlet are in their proper order before sewing.

COMBINATION
PRESS

See p. 29.

CONSERVATION
BINDING

See p. 20, 21.

CONSERVATOR

An individual who possesses the knowledge and skill to prevent or retard deterioration, and to restore deteriorated materials to a useable state.

CORDS

Heavy hemp, cotton, or linen to which *signatures* are sewn during the process of binding by hand. See tapes and *bands*.

CRASH

See *super*.

DECKLE AND SCREEN | See *mold*.

DISBINDING | Reducing a sewn book to loose *sections*, or, in the case of *adhesive binding*, to loose *leaves* by removing the entire cover, the *endpapers*, the *headbands*, the lining on the *spine* and thread. Also referred to as *pulling*.

DOUBLURE | A *pastedown* that is independent of and separate from the *flyleaf*.

DURABLE | The ability of a material to resist wear and tear.

ENCAPSULATION | To support fragile paper between two sheets of polyester film, held together by double-sided tape, machine sewing or heat seal. This preservation method does not alter the document or *leaf* in any way and is easily *reversible*.

ENCLOSURE | The term *enclosure* refers, in this manual, to various types of protective containers constructed for temporary or permanent storage of fragile, valuable library materials.

ENDPAPERS | Blank *leaves* found at the beginning and the end of a book or pamphlet. Those which swing freely are known as *flyleaves* and those which are affixed to the inside of the *boards* are known as *board sheets* or *pastedowns*.

EX LIBRIS | See *bookplate*.

FEATHERING | A fuzzy, or feathered, effect created when ink touches unsized (cf. *size*) paper.

FELT | See p. 41.

FERRULE | The metal or plastic part used to secure bristles to a brush handle.

FINISHING PRESS | See p. 29.

FLAP | The term *flap* refers, in this manual, to a broad, flexible piece of *bristol* or *paper*, projecting from a protective *enclosure*.

FLAT FILE	A cabinet containing several wide, but shallow drawers, suitable for the storage of maps, large documents, prints and other large pieces of paper.
FLYLEAF	The free-swinging portion of an *endpaper*.
FOOT	See *tail.*
FORE EDGE	The edge of a book or *pamphlet* opposite the *spine.*
FOXING	Red-brown spots that develop on paper.
GAYLORD PRESS	See p. 29.
GATHERING	See *signature.*
GRAIN	The machine direction of cloth, *board* or paper. See Chapter 5, p. 41–42.
GUARD, n.	A strip of paper or cloth on which plates are mounted or with which *signatures* are mended.
v.	To reinforce the folds of *signatures* with strips of paper.
GUTTER	The white space formed by the adjoining inside *margins* of two facing *pages*; the inner margin of a book page.
HEAD	Top of a book; particularly refers to the top of the *spine.*
HEADBAND	In early bindings, a strip of embroidery worked by hand, and used over a piece of leather or cord, at the *head* and *tail* of the *spine* of a book. In most modern books this handwork has been dispensed with and a strip of woven material is simply glued on.
HEADCAP	The covering leather that has been shaped over the *headbands* at the *head* and *tail* of the *spine* of a hand bound book.

HEAT-SET TISSUE	Very thin *lens tissue*, one side of which is coated with acrylic resin. Used for backing and *laminating* paper.
HINGE, n.	A strip of material to which a *leaf* or *tip-in* is attached.
v.	To attach one piece of paper to another by means of a narrow strip.
HOLLOW TUBE	See *tube*.
INNER MARGIN	See *gutter*.
INSERT	1. An illustration, map, plate or other item produced separately from the book, but bound into it.
	2. An extraneous item, not originally an integral part of a book that is *tipped in*.
INTERLEAVE	The term interleave is used, in this manual, to describe the insertion or placement, between *pages* or *leaves* of a text, of waxed or waste paper in order to prevent the inadvertent adhering of two surfaces or migration of moisture.
JAPANESE PAPER	Vegetable fiber paper available in various weights. Used for paper repair. Sometimes referred to as *rice paper*.
JIG	A pattern or template. Used to determine the position of holes at *sewing stations*.
JOINT	See *hinge*.
KETTLE STITCH	A knot used in sewing to firmly unite each *signature*, at the *head* and *tail*, to the preceding one.
LABEL	A piece of paper or other material, such as leather, that is printed or stamped on one side and affixed to the *spine* and/or the front cover.
LACUNA (pl., Lacunae)	A missing part or a hole in a *leaf*. Sometimes called a "loss."
LAID LINES	See p. 41.
LAMINATION	The application of *lens tissue* or *Japanese paper* to both sides of fragile paper to lend additional support. Various methods and adhesives can be used.

LEAF	One of the units which forms a *signature*, made by folding a *sheet* of paper or *vellum*. A leaf consists of the *recto*, or front and the *verso*, or back. In a text, the recto is a right-hand page.
LENS TISSUE	Very thin paper used for *lamination* and other paper repairs.
LIBRARY BINDING	A commercial method of bookbinding for libraries.
LIBRARY BOARD	A tough, sturdy, light gray color board made from selected chemical pulp. Archival and with high alkaline reserve for protection against acid deterioration. Intended for a variety of conservation applications.
LIMP BINDING	A flexible *binding* made of leather, paper or *vellum* without stiff *boards*.
LYING PRESS	See p. 29.
MAP FOLDER STOCK	Archival quality *board* with an alkaline size as an *acid* buffer.
MARGIN	The area on a *page* or *leaf* that surrounds the printed matter. The four margin areas are commonly designated: *head*, or top; *fore edge*, or outer; *tail*, or bottom; *gutter*, or inner/inside.
MARGINALIA	Handwritten notes in the *margins* of books or *pamphlets*.
MATERIAL	1. Books, *Pamphlets*, Documents, Artifacts (written or printed on paper or *vellum*) and all other items found in library collections. 2. Those substances, such as cloth, paper or *board*, used in preservation work.
METHYL CELLULOSE	See p. 44.
MICROFORMS	Microfilm, microfiche.
MICROSPATULA	A small tempered-metal spatula, flattened at both ends.
MIXTURE	In this manual, the term mixture is used to describe a combination of adhesives—usually *PVA* in combination with another adhesive such as *methyl cellulose*.

LYING PRESS — See p. 29.
METHYL CELLULOSE — See p. 44.

MOLD
: 1. Mildew, fungus.
  2. A papermaker's mold. Also referred to as a *deckle and screen*. See p. 41.

MULL
: See *super*.

NIPPING PRESS
: See p. 28. Also referred to as a copying press.

OFFSET
: Unintentional transfer of ink. Usually from the surface of a freshly printed sheet to the back of a sheet placed over it; also the ink or image transferred by printing. Also referred to as *set-off*.

OPALINE PAD
: A porous cloth bag, filled with mildly abrasive particles. Used to clean paper.

OPENABILITY
: The degree to which a book or *pamphlet* (especially one which has been rebound) may be opened flat.

OVERSEWING
: Sewing, by hand or machine, through the *spine*, or *binding edge* rather than through the fold of each *signature*, joining one to another consecutively. The sewing holes are drilled ahead of time. A similar method known as *overcasting*, differs in that each *signature* is sewn through and over the binding edge. This method is also referred to as *whipping* or *whipstitching*.

PAGE
: One side of a *leaf*.

PAMPHLET
: A book of few *pages*, issued bound in a slightly heavier (than the text) paper cover. Sometimes the term is used for any collection of *leaves* forming a unit of sixty-four pages or less.

PAMPHLET BINDING
: See p. 119.

PARCHMENT
: See *vellum*.

PASTEDOWN
: See *boardsheet*.

PASTE, n.
: 1. A vegetable-based adhesive.

v.
: 2. To apply adhesive.

PERMANENT
: Inherently stable. Intended to last indefinitely without significant alteration.

POLYESTER FILM	A chemically inert, dimensionally stable and very clear polyester sheeting used for *encapsulation*. It is available in several thicknesses, by the sheet or roll.
POLYESTER WEB	A strong, non-woven fabric, used as a support for paper when it is wet.
PRESSBOARD	A lightweight board, available in various colors. The surface appears slightly mottled and is very hard and shiny. *Pamphlet bindings* are usually made of pressboard.
PRESSING BOARDS	Flat boards of solid wood, plywood or masonite. Used on each side of a book during pressing. Often referred to simply as *boards*.
PRESSURE-SENSITIVE TAPE	See p. 39.
PULLING	See *disbinding*.
PVA	Polyvinyl Acetate. A synthetic adhesive. See p. 44.
PYROXYLIN	A nitro-cellulose compound applied to or impregnated into *book cloth* to render it moisture resistant. -*impregnated.* Pyroxylin is thoroughly forced into the base fabric, followed by additional coatings of compound over the surface. This product is then *calendered*. -*coated.* The base fabric carries a surface coating, with little penetration of the pyroxylin compound. This cloth stock is more flexible than the impregnated variety and is characterized by a leather-like appearance.
QUIRE	See *signature*.
REBACK	The process by which new cloth or other covering material is used to replace a worn out or missing *spine* and *joints*. This method reuses the original *boards*. If the original spine title is available it is frequently placed in position on the new spine covering.
RECASING LEATHER	A waterproof cloth available in rolls of different widths.

RECTO
1. The front of a *leaf* or document.
2. The righthand page of an open book; usually carrying an odd number.

REPROGRAPHY
An all inclusive term denoting a variety of processes used for copying and duplicating printed matter and photographs.

RESTORATION
See p. 20.

RICE PAPER
See *Japanese paper*.

REVERSIBLE
In this manual, the term reversible is used to denote processes which can be undone or reversed without damage to the original materials.

SADDLE STITCHING
Stitching together of a single signature pamphlet by passing thread or wire through the fold line. So called from the saddle of the stitching machine.

SCALPEL
A small knife with a very sharp blade. The blade can either be made of replaceable stainless steel or, in one piece with the handle, of carbon steel. The carbon steel blade can be honed to a fine edge.

SCORE
See p. 31, 32.

SECTION
See *signature*.

SELVAGE
The edge of a piece of fabric; finished in a manner that prevents ravelling. This portion is meant to be cut off or discarded.

SET-OFF
See *off-set*.

SEWING STATIONS
The holes, along the folds of a *signature*, through which thread passes during the sewing process.

SIGNATURE, n.
A letter or figure at the bottom of the first page of each section to facilitate in collating. Folded from one sheet of paper and trimmed on three sides to form a unit of several folded leaves with consecutive pages. Several signatures are linked by sewing. Also referred to as *section*, *quire* or *gathering*.

SPINE	The edge of the book block where the signatures are sewn together, or single leaves are attached to each other with adhesive; also that part of the cover that carries the title and author's name.
STARCH-FILLED	*Book cloth* that is coated or filled with starch. Available in many different colors, weights and textures.
SUPER	A heavily-sized cloth that resembles cheesecloth. Used to attach the *book block* to the *case*.
TAIL	The bottom of the book; particularly refers to the bottom of the *spine*.
TIP/TIP-IN	To attach an item, such as a letter, to the text of a book or *pamphlet* by painting a narrow line of adhesive along one edge of the item and affixing it to the *page, endsheet* or *pastedown*.
TRIMMER	See p. 28.
TUBE	A piece of paper that is folded to create three separate sections. The sections are folded in such a way as to create a hollow tube the exact width of the *spine*. The middle section of the tube is attached, on one side, to the spine of the book and the other two sections are affixed to each other. Also referred to as a *hollow tube*.
TURN-IN	The portion of the binding covering material that is turned over the edges of the boards toward the inside.
TWO/THREE PART FOLDER	Simple preservation *enclosures*, or containers, made either from two or three pieces of *pressboard* hinged together with strips of *book cloth*. An envelope or *bristol wrapper*, attached to the inside of one piece of pressboard, holds the book or document.

VELLUM

An animal skin that has been treated with lime and stretched and scraped rather than tanned. Used for writing, printing and for binding books. The skins are sometimes split (sliced into two layers), one layer of which is finished on both sides specifically for use as a writing material. This type of split skin, most commonly sheepskin, is called *parchment*. The terms vellum and parchment are sometimes used interchangeably.

VERSO

1. The back of a document or *page*.
2. The lefthand page of an open book; usually carrying an even number.

WHEAT PASTE

An adhesive made from wheat flour. See p. 46.

WHIPSTITCHING
(WHIPPING)

See *overcasting* (cf. *oversewing*).

WRAPPER

A simple protective *enclosure*, usually made directly around the book to insure a good fit. Constructed of either *bristol* or *mapfolder stock*.

Specialized literature, seminars and conferences have been aimed at pressing the urgency of conserving, preserving and restoring the materials in library collections. Awakening interest in and awareness of the difficulties and problems concerned with maintaining a library collection has been of paramount importance in formulating the individual plans with which each library deals with preservation problems.

Although each collection situation must be considered individually, in order that valuable time and funds not be wasted, the initial step of every preservation plan should be an assessment of the collection.

COLLECTION ASSESSMENT

In most libraries there are books, pamphlets, journals, documents, and other materials printed on paper in varying states of deterioration. As the cost of restoring and/or preserving *every* item would be beyond the means of most libraries, it is important to discriminate among these materials:

- Carefully assess the importance and condition of the items in the collection.
- Identify the various problems.
- Determine necessary treatments and assign priority.

The manner in which the assessment of a collection is undertaken usually depends on the contents and size of the collection.

For assessment purposes library materials can be categorized generally:

1. *Materials printed after 1850*: usually considered replaceable; valuable for informational or recreational content only. Distinguish between frequently used materials and those used only occasionally.

2. *Materials printed before 1850.*

3. *First editions of important works.*

4. *Presentation or association materials*: bearing unusual or important inscriptions, dedications, signatures, or marginalia.

5. *Materials that have value as artifacts or historical documents*: frequently unique or irreplaceable.

6. *Materials that are rare or extremely valuable.*

The bulk of the materials in most libraries falls within category 1.

General criteria should be established by the librarian or curator for the use and maintenance of these materials. More valuable items—those in categories 2, 3, 4, 5 and 6—should be considered and treated individually. Because there are often exceptions from these categories to the established guidelines on use and maintenance (especially for books in category 2, *those printed before 1850*), the consultation services of a reputable conservator as well as a subject specialist should be obtained in preparation for the collection assessment.

If a collection is too large to allow examination of every item, a statistical sampling may be the only realistic way to evaluate the current condition. In the libraries where it may be possible to inspect every rare and valuable item needing professional attention, a card should be prepared for each item as it is examined, giving a description, evaluating its current condition, and noting any proposed treatment.

SORTING MATERIALS ACCORDING TO PROPOSED TREATMENT

After determining the intrinsic value of the items, as well as how often they are used, grouping them according to proposed treatment will help to define preservation priorities.

All the items that are to be worked on in-house should be grouped together and flagged with strips of paper marked according to the treatment they are to receive, such as tip-ins, wrappers, encapsulation, paper repair, re-backing or pamphlet binding. Books and pamphlets should be sorted by size within their treatment groups; this is especially important for materials requiring enclosures.

Every book placed in an *enclosure* (see Ch. 8) while awaiting rebinding or restoration should be identified on the enclosure as to binding type (full leather, cloth, paper, vellum, or a combination of materials) and planned treatment. Color-coded markings on each enclosure indicating proposed treatment can simplify identification and eliminate the need to open numerous enclosures.

All items designated for treatment should be signed out to the preservation office so that they can be readily located. Finally, options to in-house treatment should be considered, these include: commercial binding, purchase of another copy or a reprint, or purchase of a microform copy.

KEEPING RECORDS

A work chart, placed in a visible and convenient location, can be used to record the number of books, pamphlets, etc., finished each month. Upon completion, each book should be dated in pencil on the lower edge of the back board, in order to gauge the lifespan of repairs and enclosures and to compile information that is needed frequently.

Rare or valuable material sent out to be restored or treated for mold, insect or water damage should be accompanied, on its return, by a detailed report of the techniques and materials employed. As a record of methods that have proven satisfactory, this report can then be consulted when seeking solutions for future problems.

After a collection is assessed and before the in-house preservation program begins, the options described in this chapter (commercial rebinding, conservation binding, restoration, and reprography) should be considered as possible adjuncts to, or in some cases substitutes for, in-house preservation.

LIBRARY BINDING

Commercial binderies offer a variety of choices for rebinding books and other materials to accommodate factors such as cost, durability, openability, aesthetics, and narrow margins. A general cut-off date for the use of library bindings should be around 1850. Books printed before 1850 are *not* usually in great demand; and if possible their original covers, endpapers, and binding structures should not be altered lest their value as historical artifacts be diminished.

During the commercial binding process, a book originally sewn *through the fold* is usually trimmed at the fold into single-leaf blocks, losing as much as one-eighth inch of the inner margin. However, if the sewing is still intact, some library binders leave the book block as is or, if necessary, resew through the fold, *on request of the librarian*. Resewing through the fold, known as Smyth sewing, enables the book to be fully opened. For frequently used books, especially those with gutter margins less than five-eighths inch wide, Smyth sewing should be considered in spite of the added expense.

Oversewing

Oversewing, or sewing through the binding edge rather than through the folds, is the sewing technique most frequently used in library binding. In order to use this method the paper must be strong, have at least a five-eighths inch gutter margin, and be flexible enough to withstand the strength test of folding a corner several times back and forth without tearing or breaking. Although oversewing creates a very strong binding, a strongly sewn book will not necessarily be durable.

Adhesive Binding (Perfect Binding)

Adhesive bindings, also referred to as perfect bindings, should be considered only as a last resort. Because of their tendency to fall apart after moderate use, they cannot be considered lasting book structures. Yet some adhesive bindings do offer certain desirable qualities:
- Minimum gutter margin requirement.
- Fairly good "openability."
- Inexpensive production cost.

Adhesive bindings are most suitable as replacement bindings on extra copies of popular books that are in great demand.

Research materials that are a permanent part of a collection should be rebound only if the binder can guarantee that the highest standards will be maintained, especially with regard to the use of durable, permanent materials. Library binding should *not* be considered as an acceptable preservation method for highly valuable, irreplaceable or unique items.

Standards for quality workmanship and materials are established by the Library Binding Institute. Copies of the "Library Binding Institute Standard for Library Binding" may be obtained by writing directly to the Institute. (See Bibliography, p. 153, for address.)

CONSERVATION BINDING

Conservation binding, a form of rebinding developed by the Library of Congress and the Newberry Library of Chicago, makes no sacrifice in terms of sound structure. Emphasis is placed on openability, durability, and economical production. These aims are achieved, in part, by using selected combinations of high-quality materials, such as linen, vellum, and hand-made 100 percent rag paper, instead of the more expensive leathers. Ornamentation, which contributes nothing to the preservation of the book, is not applied. These conservation structures resemble unadorned, simple bindings of 16th-, 17th-, and 18th century books, which have held up remarkably well.

RESTORATION

Restoration requires great skill and is costly. For this reason it is usually reserved for rare and valuable materials of artificactual value or historical importance. Where the original binding of a valuable book is patible archival quality materials should be the principal aims. Missing parts should be replaced with appropriate well-matched materials, and all replacements or restoration should be made with reversible adhesives. Whether cosmetic restoration is preferable to straightforward, or undisguised restoration is open to debate; skillfully executed, either should be acceptable. However, disguising or trying to hide repairs may imply the intention to hide what should become part of the restored material's history.

Restoration requires great skill and is costly. For this reason it is usually reserved for rare and valuable materials of artifactual value or historical importance. Where the original binding of a valuable book is unadorned and simple, rebinding by hand in the same style as the original using appropriate materials, is less expensive and a good solution. A hand bookbinder, paper restorer or conservator should perform the restoration of important materials or at the very least supervise skilled apprentices.

If restoration is deemed necessary and funds for professional restoration are not available, a sturdy preservation enclosure can offer the best alternative solution for protection.

REPROGRAPHY

Reprography, the blanket term for various forms of photographic reproduction (microfilm, microfiche, photocopy, and photographic reprint), has become an accepted preservation practice for unique, brittle and/or delicate library materials. Deteriorating texts, printed on highly acidic papers that have begun to crumble into small fragments and can no longer be handled, and materials of singular rarity alike should be copied or photographed. In most cases the original can then be safely stored, discarded or deaccessioned. Reprography can free the librarian or curator from both the burden of storing a collection of brittle materials which occupy space and draw funds away from other important items and the worry of possible theft. Because institutional policies vary on the use of reprography and the subsequent deaccession of materials, each book, pamphlet, or document should be individually considered and cleared before proceeding.

Microfilm/Microfiche

Advantages of micrographic reproduction include:
- Relative ease of duplication.
- Predicted long lifespan of the film.
- Minimal storage space requirement.

Disadvantages include:
- Loss of bibliographical evidence.
- Major expense when undertaken in-house.
- Infrequent availability of microreading machines.

What is more, receiving information on a flat screen is not a satisfactory substitute for the experience of manipulating that ingenious three-dimensional mechanical device, *the book*.

Microforms should be housed inside fireproof metal cabinets, in a controlled environment where the temperature does not exceed 70°F and the humidity is kept between 40 percent and 60 percent.

To avoid the expense of duplicating materials already on microfilm or available in reprint form, check with other libraries, commercial microfilm publishers, *Guide to Reprints*, or *Guide to Microforms in Print*. Unless a great quantity of microfilming is being considered, it may be more economically available from microfilm service agencies. For additional information on microfilming, consult the National Micrographics Association (NMA).

Photocopying

Occasionally it may be preferable to duplicate brittle texts by photocopying. Double-sided copies on archival bond paper, bound by a commercial binder, will be somewhat similar to the original book. Perhaps the best advantage offered by photocopying is that rare books can thus be made available for daily use without exposing the originals to damage from overuse, vandalism, or theft.

Photographic Reprints

In order to make a photographic reprint of a book, it may be necessary to disbind it in order to insure that the pages lie flat while being photographed. Because this requires great care, only a qualified binder should undertake both the disbinding and rebinding. If the original book will be borrowed from a library or institutional collection, the intention of the reprint publisher to disbind must be understood and approved by the curator first in order to avoid any later misunderstanding.

Note: General disbinding and rebinding instructions should be prepared by the librarian or curator; and, as each book is returned by the binder, it should be compared with the instructions and examined for quality of workmanship. Becoming familiar with binding techniques and standards will help in the preparation of binding instructions and the selection of a binder.

A preservation and repair unit can be set up with modest funding, using existing staff and space. Careful planning will help to increase potential efficiency and make optimum use of available space and materials.

WORK AREA

The perfect working space is rare indeed; most work areas must be set up in whatever space is available, under conditions that are less than ideal. In planning the preservation workshop, the three most important aspects to consider are:

1. Access to water and sink.
2. Sufficient light.
3. Adequate work and storage space.

When a potential space is located and an assessment of these factors has been made, even if the space is poor, with a bit of improvising even a poor work space can be improved without great expense.

BENCH AREA

Because the floors must be easy to keep clean, carpeting should be removed from the work bench area. If this is not possible, plexiglass sheets, such as those that are used under desks and chairs in offices, can be installed to cover this area. Each work bench area should have a table or bench whose surface is at least 2½' × 4' and stands approximately 36" high. A sturdy wooden reading room table (raised on blocks if necessary) serves as a good work bench. For comfort, chair seats should be about 8" to 10" lower than the underside of the counter or table. Inexpensive wooden bar stools (without backs) and typing chairs (with seats that can be raised high enough) are often suitable.

LIGHTING

Sufficient lighting is important; daylight is best. Light-colored walls and ceilings will help to reflect the available light. If there are no windows nearby, incandescent lighting should be available to supplement the usual fluorescent lighting.

STORAGE

Adequate storage space will help in maintaining accurate records of supplies, useful information for preparing an operating budget and eliminating duplication through accidental reordering. With adequate storage facilities work bench space can be kept free of surplus supplies and scrap material. Small tools that are used regularly should be stored close at hand in tool kits, drawers, jars, or on wall-mounted pegboard. Small quantities of items such as adhesives and mending papers should be kept conveniently near the work bench.

The main supply of bristol, bond paper, book cloth, adhesive, and all other bulk materials may be stored in a convenient closet or room. Flat files help to keep pressboard, bristol, and paper in good condition, thus eliminating waste. Along with adequate shelving, flat files should be considered a prudent investment.

Clean shelf space and/or a book truck should always be reserved for material awaiting treatment.

Institutions often have a stock of cabinets, shelves, book trucks, and other useful items tucked away in odd corners. These should be located and, if possible, pressed into service.

SUPPLIES, TOOLS AND EQUIPMENT

Supplies

An adequate program can be started with a small assortment of supplies. Acid-free bristol, bond paper, pressboard, library board, map folder stock and a variety of book cloths and adhesives are all necessary. Only small quantities of these supplies should be purchased at first. Their quality, frequency of use, and the supplier's service can then be properly evaluated before stocking them in greater quantity. Purchasing supplies in large quantity will reduce the time spent in reordering and may generate quantity discounts, a major consideration in a program budget. When budgeting permits buying in quantity, do so for only a few items at a time. By this method, a good stock of assorted colors, weights, and textures of paper and cloth, as well as other necessary supplies can be built up gradually.

Elaborate equipment and tools are not required in order to start a preservation and repair unit. *Good* equipment and tools however, will make it possible to measure, cut, sew, and paste neatly, precisely, and efficiently.

Each worker should have an individual set of hand tools, such as a bone folder, a knife, and paste brushes. This practice not only enables workers to have the tools that they prefer; it also reminds them to be careful with their chosen tools.

The list that follows itemizes essential tools and equipment, and where they can be obtained. Many items listed here are probably available from other supply houses; in this manual we often refer to specific suppliers because of our familiarity and satisfaction with their products.

Tools

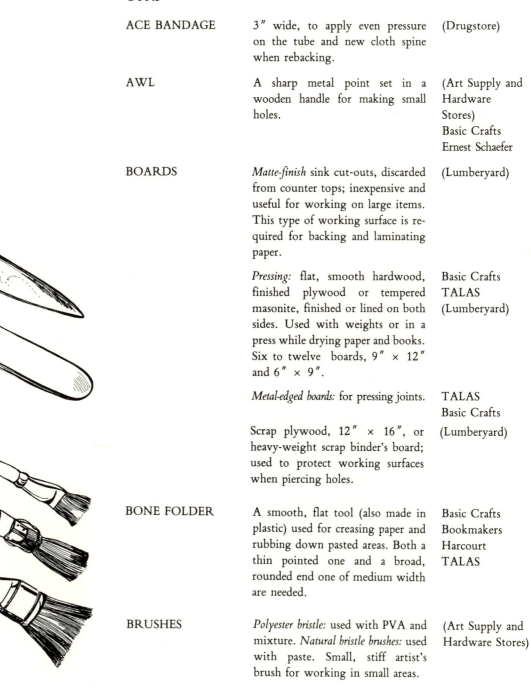

BONE FOLDERS

BRUSHES

ACE BANDAGE	3″ wide, to apply even pressure on the tube and new cloth spine when rebacking.	(Drugstore)
AWL	A sharp metal point set in a wooden handle for making small holes.	(Art Supply and Hardware Stores) Basic Crafts Ernest Schaefer
BOARDS	*Matte-finish* sink cut-outs, discarded from counter tops; inexpensive and useful for working on large items. This type of working surface is required for backing and laminating paper.	(Lumberyard)
	Pressing: flat, smooth hardwood, finished plywood or tempered masonite, finished or lined on both sides. Used with weights or in a press while drying paper and books. Six to twelve boards, 9″ × 12″ and 6″ × 9″.	Basic Crafts TALAS (Lumberyard)
	Metal-edged boards: for pressing joints.	TALAS Basic Crafts
	Scrap plywood, 12″ × 16″, or heavy-weight scrap binder's board; used to protect working surfaces when piercing holes.	(Lumberyard)
BONE FOLDER	A smooth, flat tool (also made in plastic) used for creasing paper and rubbing down pasted areas. Both a thin pointed one and a broad, rounded end one of medium width are needed.	Basic Crafts Bookmakers Harcourt TALAS
BRUSHES	*Polyester bristle:* used with PVA and mixture. *Natural bristle brushes:* used with paste. Small, stiff artist's brush for working in small areas.	(Art Supply and Hardware Stores)

BULLDOG CLIPS   See *clips.*

CARD   Used in conjunction with boards   (Library discards)
CATALOGUE   and weights to press in joints after
DRAWER RODS   rebacking.

CONTAINERS   Heavy, wide-mouthed glass jars or   (Household
                   smooth china bowls are best. Plastic discards)
                   containers should be used inside
                   larger containers to prevent spills.
                   With lids, any of these make good
                   storage containers.

CLIPS   *Bulldog or Boston:* to apply a nipping   (Art Supply and
                   or holding pressure when mending   Stationery Stores)
                   corners.

                   Paper: to keep materials aligned
                   while sewing or pasting.

ERASERS   Magic rub®, Pink Pearl®, Scum-X®   (Art Supply and
                   to remove dirt from paper. Scum-X   Stationery Store)
                   or Opaline Pad® is best for gentle
                   erasing of large surfaces.

KNIVES   *Blunt:* knife with rounded end—an   (Household
                   old table knife, unserrated, good for discards)
                   slitting paper, opening uncut pages   Basic Crafts
                   and prying open and lifting out   Bookmakers
                   staples.   TALAS.

                   Mat: also referred to as a utility
                   knife, available with replaceable
                   blades used to cut paper, board, and
                   cloth; models with a retractable
                   blade are safest.

                   Kitchen paring; best used to lift cloth
                   off boards or, when sharpened, for
                   rough cutting.

                   Scalpel: surgical scalpel with dispos-
                   able blades; handle No. 4, with
                   blade #23 for small cuts.

KNITTING   See *needles.*
NEEDLES

MALLET   A hammer with a wooden, plastic   (Art Supply Store)
                   or leather head; used with an awl to TALAS
                   make holes. A broad-headed ham-
                   mer with padding tied around the
                   head can be substituted.

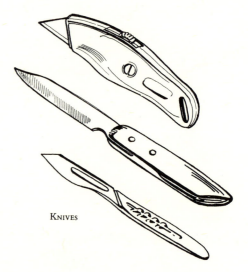

KNIVES

NEEDLES	*Knitting:* No. 3 metal needles for applying adhesive to tighten cases and for pressing down joints. *Sewing:* cotton darner #3-00. *Crewel:* for sewing signatures and pamphlets.	(Sewing Store) Basic Craft Bookmakers Gaylord TALAS
PANS	Plastic photographic trays, glass, enamel or stainless steel baking pans; used for soaking or washing papers.	(Household supplies, Photo Supply Store, Supermarket)
PAPER CLIPS	See *clips.*	
RAGS	Cotton, flannel or worn terry cloth are best, use dampened to clean fingers and to remove excess paste.	(Household discards)
RULERS	*Plastic:* see-through 6″ and 12″ rulers for measuring. *Steel or aluminum:* 12″ and 18″ lengths for measuring and/or cutting guides.	(Art Supply Store) (Hardware Store) Basic Crafts TALAS
SCALPEL	See *knives.*	
SCISSORS	Medium size, with pointed tips and of good quality.	(Sewing Store) TALAS
SHARPENING STONE	With a fine and a medium side for sharpening knife blades.	(Hardware Store)
SPATULA	Aluminum or steel microspatulas for fine work where it would be dangerous to use a sharp tool.	TALAS
STRAIGHT-EDGE	Heavy steel, 24″ to 36″ long; used as a guide when cutting with a mat knife or scoring with a bone folder.	(Art Supply Store) (Hardware Store) Basic Crafts TALAS
TRIANGLE	A 6″ or larger 45–90 degree triangle; used to check square of corners when measuring and cutting.	(Art Supply Store)
WEIGHTS	Small, heavy items such as bricks, pieces of cast iron or lead, wrapped in paper and secured with tape, and containers filled with lead shot. Used to prevent curling and warping, and to prevent shifting of materials.	Building material supplies, Hardware Store Discards

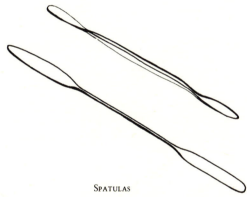

Spatulas

Equipment: Cutters and Trimmers

The single most expensive piece of equipment is a cutter. A good cutter is a one-time investment that will not require any maintenance other than blade sharpening, approximately every five years. A cutter not only makes many jobs easier—such as the making of enclosures, for example—but improves accuracy and efficiency.

The cutter selected should have a clamp or pressure bar. This bar holds the sheet of paper or board firmly in position on the cutter bed while the cut is being made. To accommodate very large sheets the pressure bar can be moved out of the way. It is the pressure bar that marks the difference between this type of cutter and the less expensive office models. The next most important features are gauges, of which the preferred cutters usually have two. One gauge is positioned to the left of and parallel to the cutting edge; it can be moved along a guide marked in inches. The other gauge, positioned to the right of and parallel to the cutting edge, is called the outside or rollout gauge. This gauge holds large sections in an even position and is also helpful when cutting a quantity of narrow, even strips.

A less expensive and less versatile cutter is called a *trimmer*. Operating on a different principle from the cutters described above, the trimmer consists of a long bed with a clamp and bar arrangement on the right side and a circular cutting head containing a small wheel-shaped knife which cuts as it travels along the bar.

Trimmers will cut paper, bristol, and press board, but should not be used to cut binder's board. Some trimmers are equipped with a pressure bar, but *all* trimmers lack adjustable gauges.

Equipment: Presses

A press is not essential, but it is a convenient piece of equipment. Some libraries have presses that have been donated or acquired and are now stored away and forgotten. A press found and rescued or purchased will stand a preservation workshop in good stead.

NIPPING PRESS

The nipping press is the most commonly found type of press. It is made of iron and quite indestructible. A nipping press can facilitate the making of more extensive repair work and, because of its size, can be easily stored when not in use.

GAYLORD PRESS

The Gaylord press is another type frequently found in use in libraries. Consisting of an iron pipe and a screw mechanism for clamping boards together, the Gaylord press opens wide enough to add extra masonite boards, permitting a number of books to be pressed at the same time.

LYING PRESS

The lying press is a heavy press used for holding a book firmly in position while freeing both hands to work on the spine. This press is usually made of hardwood with wooden screws at each end for tightening or loosening the cheeks, but variant types are made of metal with a central screw mechanism. Used in conjunction with a tub (a four-legged stand), the lying press can be elevated to accommodate a book, placed fore edge down, without its coming into contact with a hard surface.

FINISHING PRESS

The main function of the finishing press is to hold a book firmly in position, leaving both hands free to work. Because it is deeper and lighter in weight than the lying press (making it easier to handle), this press is particularly useful when cleaning or working on the spine and edges of a book.

COMBINATION PRESS

One simplified version of the combination press consists of two pieces of three-quarter-inch plywood held together, and apart, by two carriage bolts with wing nuts. A strip of brass is attached to one long edge of each board so that approximately one-sixteenth inch of the brass strip extends toward the inside of the press. The brass edges are used to set, or form, the joints of books.

These tips are included to make it easier to begin working and to help economize on both time and materials.

MEASURING

To measure and cut one piece of paper, cloth, or board quickly and accurately to the same dimensions as another, it is seldom necessary to measure with a ruler. Instead, simply place the original item or material on the piece to be cut and, using a pencil, mark the place where the cut should be made.

Another convenient method uses a narrow strip of scrap paper instead of a ruler. The strip of paper is placed on or next to the book, board, or whatever the original is, and the required dimension is marked along the strip. The mark is then transferred from the strip to the material that is to be cut. If the measurement taken is to be divided, simply fold the strip into equal parts (e.g., halves, thirds). The folded strip can then be used to mark accurate divisions on the material to be cut. (see Figure 1).

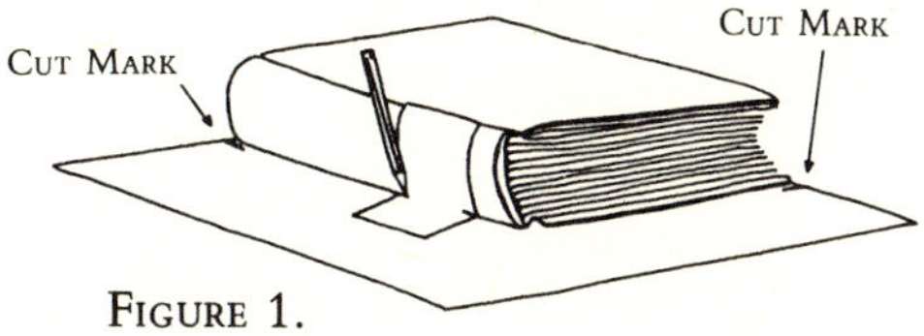

CUT MARK   CUT MARK

FIGURE 1.

SCORING, CREASING AND FOLDING

Although it is much easier to fold paper or bristol in the direction of the *grain* — or with the grain as it is called — (see Chapter 5 for methods of determining grain direction), folds made against the grain can still be made neatly, with a little practice, using a bone folder.

Folding a Large Sheet

To fold a large sheet of bristol or paper in half, place it in front of you so that the fold will run parallel to the edge of the work surface. Double the sheet over away from you and bring the four corners exactly together. In order to free your hands to make the fold (while the edges are held evenly in position), hold the end edges down with weights (wrapped bricks) or a heavy straightedge. Place your left hand on the sheet and press the fold down using your left thumb. Now, starting in the middle, crease the sheet by drawing a bone folder smoothly across the fold to the right and off the end of the sheet. Then draw it from the middle to the left and off the sheet. (see Figure 2).

FIGURE 2.

Scoring

To make a sharply creased fold on bristol, first *score* it where the fold will be made. To score, make a small mark at each end of the sheet and align a straightedge on the marks. Pressing down firmly (on both straightedge and bone folder), draw the sharp end of a bone folder along the side of the straightedge. Holding the straightedge in position, place the bone folder under the bristol and fold it up against the side of the straightedge. (see Figure 3).

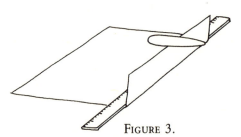

FIGURE 3.

Folding with a Cutter

Using a cutter equipped with a clamp and pressure bar, a good fold on bristol or other material of similar weight can be made in one operation. Make a small mark (to indicate the position of the fold) at each edge of the material. Align the material in the cutter as if you were going to cut at the mark. Leave the blade *up* and lower the pressure bar. Bend the material down against the edge of the cutter, using a bone folder. (see Figure 4).

CUTTING

Right-Angle Cutting/Squaring

To obtain a right angle cut or to square the corners of paper, board, or cloth, one edge must be held flush against the bottom guide of the cutter. When the material is in place it should be held firmly by the pressure bar. Simple office cutters, which are not equipped with pressure bars or clamps of any kind, permit the material to slip out of position as the blade is lowered.

FIGURE 4.

Cutting Materials to a Uniform Size Using a Jig

To easily cut pieces of material of equal dimension as one that has already been cut, use the original as a jig. Lower the blade of the cutter and place the original piece (the jig) under the pressure bar until its right edge is stopped against the lowered blade. Adjust the lefthand gauge so that it is against the left edge of the original piece and tighten. Leaving the gauge in place, remove the original piece and insert the new material so that one edge is against the lefthand gauge, and cut. The new piece will have the same measurement as the original that was used as a pattern.

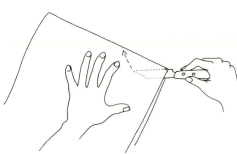

FIGURE 5.

Quick Cutting Oversize Sheets

To cut a sheet of paper, bristol or cloth that is too big for the cutter, fold the desired amount over and, as explained in the section on folding and creasing, sharply crease the fold. Insert a kitchen knife at an angle into the fold. Moving the knife in a smooth outward motion against the fold, cut in the direction away from yourself. Avoid using a sawing motion. This method can be accomplished more quickly than drawing pencil lines, using a straightedge, and cutting with scissors. (see Figure 5).

Dividing an Oversize Sheet Equally Using a Cutter

If a large sheet is to be divided into several smaller pieces of the same dimension, it is more efficient to use the cutter. Fold the sheet to approximate the needed size being careful to note the grain direction. Square by placing the fold against the bottom cutter guide and trim. Place the trimmed edge against the guide and square the next corner. Continue in the same manner until all edges are trimmed and corners squared. (see Figure 6).

FIGURE 6A.

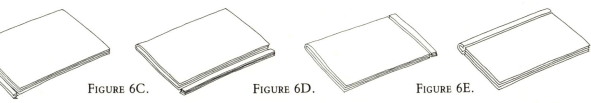

FIGURE 6B.   FIGURE 6C.   FIGURE 6D.   FIGURE 6E.

Cutting Pressboard

On some cutters, the pressure bar can be positioned up, out of the way, to permit the cutting of rigid board such as pressboard. A sheet of pressboard that is longer than the cutting edge can be cut (as illustrated below) in two steps.

Step 1. Place the pressboard on the cutter near the hinge of the blade, with the top edge flush against the top guide. Then bring the blade down until approximately two-thirds of the sheet length is cut. It is better to make the first cut oversize (see Figure 7).

Step 2. After the first cut is made lift the blade and reverse the pressboard so that the uncut edge is aligned at the hinge and then lower the blade to the point of the first cut. This method does not always produce an accurate cut, but it is a good way to reduce a large piece of board to a manageable size (see Figure 7).

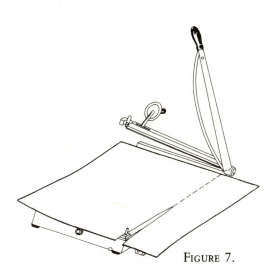

FIGURE 7.

Cutting Narrow Strips

Cutting narrow strips of equal dimension is made easier, and more efficient, with a cutter that is equipped with a righthand or rollout gauge.(see Figure 8).

1. First set the gauge to the desired width of the strip.
2. Then place the material that is to be cut under the pressure bar until it touches the gauge.
3. Lower the blade and cut.
4. Raise the blade and move the material further under the pressure bar until it again touches the gauge.
5. Continue this process until the desired number of strips are cut.

FIGURE 8.

If the cutter is not equipped with a rollout gauge, narrow strips can be cut using the following method:

1. Set and tighten the lefthand gauge to a distance of six inches *plus* the width of the required strip from the cutting edge.
2. Cut a piece of pressboard six inches wide by the length of the cutter bed and fit it snugly against the lefthand gauge.
3. Place the material to be cut under the pressure bar so that the edge is adjacent to the edge of the pressboard strip.
4. Lower the bar and cut off the required strip.

Cutting Narrow Strips by Hand

To cut narrow strips by hand, first bring the corners of the material together but *do not crease*. Then, hold the materials in position with a ruler and using an awl or dividers make small holes along the ruler edge in increments equal to the width of the required strips through *both* layers. Unfold the sheet and position a straightedge between the corresponding holes on either side. Press firmly on the straightedge and, using a scalpel, an x-acto knife, or a mat knife, cut (using a light stroke) several times. Cutting lightly insures that the blade will follow the straightedge and not be diverted, ruining the cut or possibly causing injury. (see Figures 9 and 10).

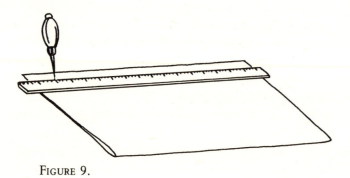

FIGURE 9.

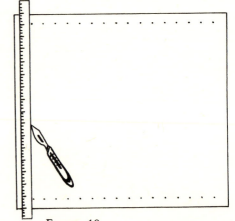

FIGURE 10.

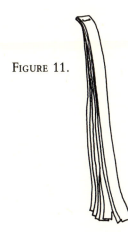

Figure 11.

Thin paper, especially Japanese paper, can be cut several layers at a time, using a cutter or a knife and straightedge. A group of strips should be stapled together at one end and placed conveniently at hand; then single strips can be pulled off as needed. (see Figure 11).

PASTING

Preparing the Work Surface

Before beginning a project that requires pasting, collect a supply of waste paper. An old telephone directory will provide small sheets. Unprinted newsprint, which can sometimes be obtained free of charge from newspaper offices (ask for end rolls), will cover large areas well. Printed newspapers should be a last resort and—because the ink rubs off easily, causing staining—should be used with care.

Preparing the Adhesive

The next step is to prepare the adhesive. The adhesive should be stored in a separate, clean container with a tight cap. From this container small amounts can be poured into a small bowl or wide-mouth jar as required, thereby eliminating the need to dip the brush back into the main supply of adhesive and possibly contaminating it. Scraping the brush onto only one side of the bowl or jar will keep an area clean for resting the brush handle. As an added precaution, a damp cotton rag should be kept handy in a small saucer for cleaning adhesive from hands as well as handles. (see Figure 12).

Figure 12.

Applying the Adhesive

Learning to apply the correct amount of adhesive is very important. An evenly applied thin coating is best. The bond is *not* made stronger by additional paste, mixture, or PVA. Besides being uneven, a thick coating is likely to be forced out at the edges when pressure or weight is applied. A thick layer of adhesive will dry slowly and allow moisture to seep into other areas, possibly cockling the paper.

Pasting Defined Areas

A good example of pasting a defined, limited area is the application of adhesive to the edge of a *leaf* that is to be *hinged* or *tipped* in.
1. Place the leaf on the waste paper.
2. Lay another strip of waste paper over the leaf exposing only the area to be pasted.
3. Apply the adhesive, moving from the top layer of waste paper to the leaf and then to the bottom layer of waste paper. (see Figure 13).
4. Carefully remove the waste paper and affix the pasted leaf.

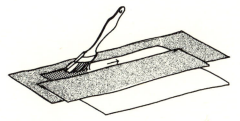

Figure 13.

Pasting Large Pieces

1. To apply adhesive to a large piece of paper or cloth, first place the piece on a larger sheet of waste paper.
2. Holding the piece of cloth or paper in the center securely with one hand, using quick long strokes, brush a thin layer of adhesive from the center *out* onto the waste paper. (see Figure 14).
3. Shift the position of your fingers in order to cover the area completely. Note: *Never* brush adhesive starting from the waste paper and moving toward the center of the paper or cloth lest it get underneath the material onto the front side, creating a stain. Before handling the pasted piece, be sure to clean any paste from your fingers with the damp cotton rag.

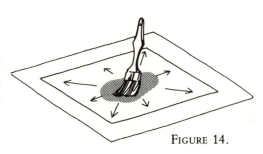

FIGURE 14.

PRESSING

Of the presses described in Chapter 3, a *combination press* is the most useful. In lieu of a combination press, *weights* (bricks wrapped in several layers of brown paper to eliminate dust) and *boards* (rectangular pieces of plywood or masonite, approximately 9″ × 12″) will serve for most purposes. Although bricks are brittle and easily broken if dropped, they are good, inexpensive weights. Easily cleaned pressing boards can be made from inexpensive, Formica-covered sink cutouts left over from kitchen counter installations. These can be bought at most local lumberyards.

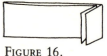

FIGURE 15.

FIGURE 16.

MAKING NEW SEWING HOLES USING A JIG

If the existing holes in a book or pamphlet become enlarged or torn, making them unusuable for resewing, new holes can easily be made. Use the following method to make a pattern, or jig, for determining the distance between the new *sewing stations*. (For side sewing see note.)

1. Cut a three-inch wide strip of heavy paper or bristol, equal to the height of the text block, and fold it in half (see Figure 15).
2. Leave it folded, and make a fold about one-half inch from *each* end (see Figure 16).
3. Then bring the middle fold over to meet the folds half an inch from the end. Crease the new fold (see Figure 17).
4. Unfold the strip.
5. Next, fold the strip *lengthwise* in half (see Figure 18).
6. Pierce the intersections of the folds with an awl or needle and cut a small notch in one short edge of the jig (see Figure 19).

FIGURE 17.

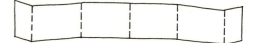

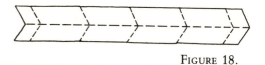

FIGURE 18.

FIGURE 19.

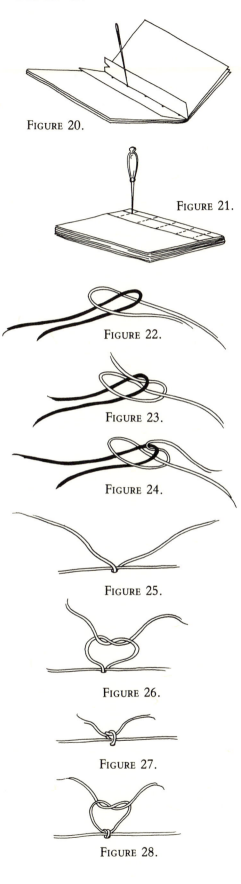

FIGURE 20.

FIGURE 21.

FIGURE 22.

FIGURE 23.

FIGURE 24.

FIGURE 25.

FIGURE 26.

FIGURE 27.

FIGURE 28.

7. Insert the jig into each signature, with the notch always on the same side.
8. Pierce through the signature folds, using the jig to position the holes. Exact positioning of the holes in the fold of each signature will result in straight sewing. (see Figure 20).

Note: When side sewing (see Chapter 9), position the folded jig one-fourth inch to three-eighths inch away from the spine edge of the book or pamphlet and make pencil marks at the vertical folds of the jig. Using an awl or needle, pierce through the signatures at these pencil marks. (see Figure 21).

TYING KNOTS

Tying On a New Piece of Thread

In the course of sewing a book made up of multiple signatures, it is often necessary to tie on a new piece of thread. The knotting method used in this process can be accomplished easily. It is important to tie the knot close to the last sewing station so that the thread will not have any slack as it enters the next sewing station.

1. Make a loop of the remaining thread and hold it in your left hand, with the short end of the loop on the bottom.
2. With a new thread, make a loop with the short end on the bottom and hold it in your right hand.
3. Insert the left-hand loop underneath and *into* the right-hand loop and hold both in place with your left thumb (Figure 22).
4. Take the short end of the right-hand loop under and through the left-hand loop as illustrated (Figure 23).
5. Pull the short end of the left-hand loop and both ends of the right-hand loop away from each other until the knot is secure (Figure 24). Trim the ends.

Finishing Knot for a Single Signature (Square Knot)

As the threads come out of the center station, they will be on either side of the middle thread section (Figure 25).

1. Take one end in each hand.
2. Pass the right-hand thread over the left-hand thread and through the loop. Pull tight (Figure 26, 27).
3. The *original* right-hand thread is now on the left side (see Figure 28). Place it over the thread and bring through the loop. Pull tight. Trim the ends.

CARE AND CLEANING OF TOOLS

Brushes

Expensive brushes are not necessary for most preservation work. Polyester-bristle or nylon-bristle paint brushes from a hardware store are suitable and will, with simple care, last a long time. Round natural-bristle glue brushes, available through bookbinding supply house catalogs (see Supply Sources, pp. 147–148), are suitable for use with *paste*. These natural-bristle brushes are *not* recommended for use with *polyvinyl acetate* (PVA), however, because it is particularly difficult to clean PVA out of this kind of brush. Paste and *methyl cellulose* can be washed out of brushes quite easily, but PVA if allowed to harden, is extremely difficult to remove.

To reclaim a brush that has hardened PVA in it, soak the brush for several days and then remove the bits of PVA. If you decide to undertake this project, a fine-tooth comb will help; however, the task is time-consuming.

Used brushes should be washed thoroughly with hot water and detergent and rinsed well. If there is not enough time to wash brushes well, place them in a jar of water. Brushes should always be *in* the adhesive, or *in* water, or completely washed out when not in use. Brushes that are to be used again within a few hours can be left in the adhesive, with their bristles well covered. After washing, always hang brushes with their bristles down. This will prevent the ferrule from becoming clogged.

Avoid long-handled brushes; although they appear elegant, they *are* unwieldy and, in use, may cause the adhesive container to tip over. Cut the wooden handle to a convenient length and if necessary cover the end with tape.

Bone Folders

SEALING: To prepare bone folders (except those made of plastic) for use, place them in a vegetable oil bath overnight. This process seals the bone folder, giving it a polished surface that helps to decrease drag when creasing paper. This sealing will also make it easy to wash off dye discoloration or adhesive that has been transferred from bookcloth.

RESHAPING: Because bone folders are easily broken, they should never be used to pry open containers or as a substitute for a screwdriver. Should the end of a bone folder chip or break, it can be reshaped with a file and finished with extra-fine sandpaper.

Knives

A good edge can be maintained on knives by the correct and frequent use of a sharpening stone. The stone should be oiled when it is new; after a while water can be used in place of oil. To sharpen the knife, hold the blade flat against the stone and stroke it, using a circular motion. Lift the blade up and off on the return stroke. The last few strokes should be very light to avoid creating any burrs on the blade edge. When the blade is sharp, stroke the unbeveled side on the smooth side of the stone once or twice lightly to remove burrs created in the sharpening process. Knives beveled on only one side should be sharpened, or honed, only on that side, whereas knives beveled on both sides should be honed on both sides.

MENDING TAPES

Do not use pressure-sensitive tape on paper or bookcloth, even if the manufacturer advertises that it is made especially for books or if it is sold as permanent, invisible, or magic. These tapes usually dry out, stain paper, gum up cloth, shrink, and ooze at the sides.

The preservation problems resulting from the use of these tapes are often worse than the original tears. The removal of these tapes and tape stains should be left to an experienced conservator.

Note: to all rules there are exceptions, and, as of this writing there are only two. The acceptable mending tapes are:

- Ademco® Archival Repair Tape
- Filmo-plast®

Both Ademco and Filmo-plast are thin, transparent and acid-free for making paper repairs, reversible (Ademco in ethyl alcohol and Filmo-plast in water).

PAPER CLIPS, STAPLES AND RUBBER BANDS

Another item to avoid is the ordinary metal paper clip, which can rust and stain paper after a short while. Plastic clips are safer than the metal ones and should be substituted where a clip is necessary. Because staples also rust, remove them from pamphlets that are to be preserved and replace them with simple sewing.

When separated parts of a book or pamphlet must be kept together temporarily, without using a preservation enclosure, do not give in to the temptation to use a rubber band. It will cut into the boards or shred brittle or loose pages that project beyond the fore-edge. Disintegrating rubber bands give off sulfur, which will eventually harm the material you are trying to preserve. When a rubber band seems appropriate, it would be better to tie up the item carefully with quarter-inch cotton tape.

5 | PHYSICAL PROPERTIES OF PAPER, ADHESIVES AND BOOKCLOTH

PAPER

In order to understand the physical properties of paper, it is necessary to understand how paper is, and has been, made.

Until the early nineteenth century, when machinery for making paper was invented, each sheet was formed by hand. In the western world this process begins with the making of the pulp fibers into a *slurry*, which is done by suspending the macerated fibers in water in a deep vat. Although pulp can be made of fibrous materials from many sources — and by many methods — linen rags have long been used in the western world to make pulp for fine hand-made paper. As the available supply of linen rag has decreased, cotton rags and linters, a by-product of ginning, have been substituted. (Paper is also made by hand from cellulose fibers such as grass, esparto, straw, as well as from kozo, mulberry, and gampi, with which the Japanese make excellent paper.)

A portion of the slurry is scooped from the vat using a mold known as a *deckle and screen*, made up of two wooden frames, one of which contains a mesh screen of thin brass wires. This screen composed of vertical wires spaced about an inch apart, causes the formation of vertical *chain lines* and horizontal *laid lines* in the finished sheets.

When a slurry is scooped out of the vat with the mold, a series of left-to-right and forward-to-backward hand and arm motions interlock the fibers and form the sheet. During this procedure the excess water drains off. At this point the deckle is removed and the sheet is transferred, or couched, onto a heavy blanket, known as a *felt*. Then it is covered over with another felt. After a post, made up of a quantity of sheets and felts is formed, it is ready to be placed into a press. These last two steps — couching and pressing — further consolidate the fibers, producing paper that is flexible and durable and shows little or no evidence of *grain*.

With the advent of mechanized paper-making, the character of paper changed. Mechanization made possible the fabrication of a continuous sheet of paper that could be cut into sheets. The paper made in this manner possesses a significant characteristic — more distinct *grain* and *cross grain*. Their degree of prominence greatly affects the paper's ability to be folded.

Since the middle of the nineteenth century, machine-made paper has generally been manufactured using wood pulp fibers. Because of availability and cost factors, wood pulp has continued to be considered the most practical fibrous material for the manufacture of commercial-grade papers.

To prevent ink from penetrating the paper's surface and spreading or feathering, early papermakers dipped each finished sheet into a bath containing a mucilaginous substance, made from animals, known as *size*. In order to prevent the animal sizing from putrifying, *alum* was added. By the early nineteenth century, both alum and rosin were being added to the pulp itself as internal sizing.

The addition of alum and rosin, as well as other chemicals such as chlorine bleach, along with the use of mechanically ground wood fibers, increased the acidity of the finished paper.

Grain Direction

A fold or crease made with the grain of paper will be sharp and accurate, whereas one made against the grain may be rough and may damage the fibers, thereby causing tears or breaks. In the binding, repairing, and restoration of library materials, *all* fibrous substances incorporated into the original structure should have their fiber direction, or grain, running parallel to the spine. (see Figure 29).

Paper bound into a book with the grain running from spine to foredge will not respond properly to atmospheric changes and may wrinkle or *cockle* as it pulls and stretches, whereas paper bound with the grain running parallel to the spine will permit the book to open easily and the pages to lie flat under their own weight. (see Figure 30).

Determining Grain Direction

The grain direction of some types of paper, such as mold-made, can be determined by holding a sheet up to light to discern the direction of the chain lines, spaced approximately one inch apart. The grain of mold-made paper runs parallel to the chain lines.

Where the chain lines are not visible, another method used with both paper and board, must be employed to help determine grain direction.

Take a sheet and bend it over. Try it first in one direction then in the other, but do not make a crease. Press down lightly and observe the degree of resistance. The bend that resists *less* when lightly pressed has the grain running parallel to it, whereas the bend that encounters greater resistance is against the grain, or cross grain. (see Figure 31).

If the grain direction is still not obvious, another method can be used. In fibrous material such as paper, a tear in the direction of the grain is *straighter* and meets with less resistance than a tear made against the grain. (see Figure 32).

Some machine-made papers are *wove* and have no chain lines. When folded or creased with the grain, these papers offer little resistance, whereas when folded against the grain, they resist and may even crack. For wove paper, another method, such as moistening, is helpful in determining grain direction. When a small square of paper is moistened, the fibers relax, swell, and stretch in the cross grain direction,

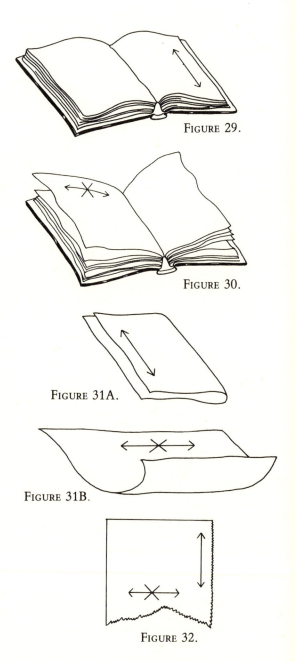

FIGURE 29.

FIGURE 30.

FIGURE 31A.

FIGURE 31B.

FIGURE 32.

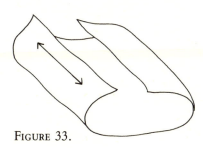

FIGURE 33.

causing the paper to curl into a cylindrical-shaped tube. The grain runs parallel to the length of this tube. (see Figure 33).

BOOK CLOTH

Two basic types of book covering cloth are most frequently used on books: *starch-filled* and *Pyroxylin-impregnated*. Familiarity with the two types will help in recognizing the differences between them. *Pyroxylin-impregnated book cloth* can be cleaned by wiping it with a damp cloth, whereas *starch-filled book cloth* cannot be dampened because the sizing will lift off and the color will run.

Book cloth can be tested by rubbing a slightly moistened cotton swab over a small area in an inconspicuous place, such as the back cover or the turn-in. If color comes off or becomes tacky, *stop*—the cloth is *starch-filled*. If there is any doubt at all, do not attempt any cleaning that involves moisture, lest the moisture seep under the cloth and loosen it from the binder's board.

The methods used to clean paper can also be used to clean starch-filled cloth. (see p. 51).

ADHESIVES

In this manual the term *adhesive* denotes pastes, glues, man-made polyvinyl acetate (PVA) and methyl cellulose.

Pastes

All pastes have a vegetable origin (as does methyl cellulose) and are a mixture of water and flour or starch. The flour can be wheat, rice, or cornstarch. Some flours are precooked and need only be mixed with water, while others must be cooked before use.

Glues

Glues, derived from animal products, must be used hot. Because many facilities do not have the equipment for making glue, such as a carefully regulated heat source, glue is referred to only occasionally in this manual.

Synthetic Adhesives

Synthetic (or man-made) adhesives, such as PVA, appear under a variety of trade names. They are usually either mixed or thinned with water. Epoxy adhesives, which are not water-based, are to be avoided. Like rubber cement, epoxy will dry out and indelibly stain paper.

The charts on the following pages describe adhesives most commonly used in preservation work, detailing their uses, characteristics and availability. All the adhesives listed are mixed with water. Brushes and containers used with them can be cleaned with water.

PROPERTIES OF ADHESIVES

All can be mixed with water; brushes and dishes can be cleaned in water.

Name of Adhesive	Setting Time	Flexibility	Reversibility	Causes Paper to Stretch
PVA (polyvinyl acetate.) *Trade names:* Elvace® Jade 403®, Promatco® A-1023®, Magic Mend®, Elmer's®, Sobo®, etc.	Fast	Quite flexible	Is usually not reversible in water. When mixed with flour paste or methyl cellulose (see below), PVA is more water soluble.	Slightly
METHYL CELLULOSE	Slow	Quite flexible	Easily removed with water.	Moderately; More than PVA and less than paste.

(The addresses for all suppliers listed can be found on pp. 147–148, Supply Sources.)

Method of Preparation	Keeps or Spoils	Appropriate Uses	Other Characteristics	Available From
Pour into small container and thin with water to desired brushing consistency.	Keeps well for at least several months. Do not allow contents to freeze. Never dip brush into main supply, as this may cause contamination	Pamphlet binders, folders, wrappers; straight PVA is not suitable for paper repairs. Use when a flexible fast-drying adhesive is desired and reversibility is not particularly important.	All PVA's are white liquids. Formulas differ in drying time, degree of reversibility, acidity, chemical stability, thickness and other properties, incl. shelf life. PVA stains are very difficult to remove when dry.	Bookmakers, Gaylord, Process Materials, TALAS, hardware store.
Stir 2 tsps. into 1 cup water; let stand one hour stirring occasionally. This can be thinned with water if desired.	Keeps well at room temperature for months after mixing.	Useful for cleaning spines and removing labels. Makes a very smooth *mixture* when combined with PVA.	Granular powder mixed with water to make a translucent substance. Does not have strong bonding qualities.	New York Central Supply TALAS. Process Materials

PROPERTIES OF ADHESIVES

All can be mixed with water; brushes and dishes can be cleaned in water.

Name of Adhesive	Setting Time	Flexibility	Reversibility	Causes Paper to Stretch
PASTE pre-cooked flour paste, also, rice starch, corn starch, or wheat flour.)	Slow	Fairly flexible if applied thinly; stiffer when thick.	Easily removed with water.	Substantially; especially if the paste is thin.
MIXTURE	Slower than PVA, but much faster than paste.	Quite flexible	More or less reversible in water depending on the type of PVA used.	Moderately; More than PVA and less than paste.

(The addresses for all suppliers listed can be found on pp. 147–148, Supply Sources.)

Method of Preparation	Keeps or Spoils	Appropriate Uses	Other Characteristics	Available From
Pre-cooked flour paste: sprinkle powder into water, while beating until right consistency for intended use. *Rice starch, corn starch or wheat flour:* Sprinkle approx. one part flour into ten parts water. Stir constantly and boil gently for about 5 minutes until translucent. Strain thru cheesecloth to eliminate lumps.	Molds very quickly; can be kept for at least a week if refrigerated between uses. If it thickens, thin by adding extra water.	Pasting end-sheets, most types of paper repairs; loosening and removing old labels, bookplates, etc. and for cleaning old glue from spines. Can be used for covering cases and boxes. Mix with PVA for a quicker drying adhesive.	Pre-cooked flour paste; the prepared paste is somewhat gritty. Can be strained thru cheesecloth. Rice, corn or wheat flour make extremely smooth pastes and have been used safely for centuries. Paste can usually be wiped off with damp cotton.	*Pre-cooked dry paste:* Bookmakers, TALAS. *Mixed, ready-to-use:* Harcourt. *Corn starch & wheat flour:* supermarket *Rice starch:* TALAS or oriental food store.
Mix PVA with paste *or* methyl cellulose. Can be made thinner with water. (Approximate percentages for different uses vary to suit working pace.)	If made with methyl cellulose, it keeps very well at room temp. Mixture made with paste spoils, unless refrigerated between uses.	Pamphlet binders, folders, wrappers, slip cases, boxes, applying labels, rebacking.	Excellent all around adhesive.	Bookmakers, TALAS, Basic Crafts, Harcourt, Gaylord, New York Central Supply, Process Materials.

PROPERTIES OF ADHESIVES

All can be mixed with water; brushes and dishes can be cleaned in water.

Name of Adhesive	Setting Time	Flexibility	Reversibility	Causes Paper to Stretch
HOT ANIMAL GLUE	Fast	Fairly flexible if applied thinly.	Easily removed with water. Can be softened and reshaped by moistening or reheating.	Moderately.
FLEXIBLE GLUE	Much slower than reg. hot glue.	Quite flexible.	Similar to above.	Causes paper to stretch less than regular hot glue.

(The addresses for all suppliers listed can be found on pp. 147–148, Supply Sources.)

Method of Preparation	Keeps or Spoils	Appropriate Uses	Other Characteristics	Available From
Heat about ½ cup granules and 1 cup water together for about 15 minutes. When this has dissolved, thin with water to desired consistency. Use a glue pot, double boiler, or a jar in a pan of simmering water.	Spoils in a few days, unless refrigerated between uses or reheated frequently.	Suitable for gluing up spines and gluing cloth or paper to binder's board. Not appropriate for paper repairs.	Must be applied thinly to be flexible, otherwise it cracks. If overheated, glue burns and smells foul, and becomes brittle and dark.	Harcourt
This glue comes in a gelatinous block and is mixed by heating a piece of it with sufficient water to obtain desired consistency.	Similar to above.	Similar to above.	The slower drying time and weaker pull are due to a high glycerin content. Other properties are similar to above.	Basic Crafts, Harcourt, TALAS.

The solution to several preservation problems dealing with paper cleaning and repair, such as soiled pages, flattening creases, uncut book pages, and repairing, backing and laminating paper have been grouped together in this section. The procedures are simple, and with care and patience they can be carried out well.

CLEANING PAPER COVERS

Materials and Tools:
1. Opaline Pad
2. Soft bristle brush
3. Gauze or soft cloth
4. Pink Pearl eraser
5. Cotton swabs

Release cleaning granules from an Opaline pad onto the paper by rotating and pressing the pad between the palms of your hands. Gently rub the granules across the cover with your fingertips. As the granules absorb the dirt and darken, brush them off with a soft brush or gauze, making sure that all are removed.

Gently rubbing a Pink Pearl eraser across the paper is another way to remove dirty spots or smudges. Be careful with paper-covered books, because excessive rubbing can remove the surface of the paper.

CLEANING PRINTED LEAVES/PAGES

The following instructions are intended for use in cleaning only printed leaves or pages of a book. Do not attempt to clean works of art on paper in this way. Paint, charcoal, and pastels have their own inherent properties and should be left to the expertise of a professional art restorer.

Materials and Tools:
1. Opaline pad
2. Pink Pearl eraser
3. Index card or 5 mil Mylar
4. Soft brush

Before attempting to clean paper, *carefully* consider the condition of each individual sheet or leaf. Brittle paper should not be cleaned, as abrasive action can cause it to crumble or tear. However, if the paper is only slightly soiled and otherwise in good condition, it can be cleaned with an Opaline pad. Heavily soiled leaves, dirty smudges, or pencil marks can usually be removed with a Pink Pearl eraser.

Any kind of soil removal must be undertaken with care, using a light touch. Always work from the center of the page toward the edge. When erasing along the edges of a page, it is advisable to support the edge with an index card or a similar piece of 5 mil Mylar to prevent tearing. Erase in small sections *toward the edge* of the page onto the support. After each portion is completed, move the support and proceed to the next area. Particles from the eraser should be swept from the page and the gutter margin with a soft brush.

FLATTENING CREASES IN PAPER

Materials and Tools:
1. Scrap board
2. Cotton swabs
3. Untextured white blotter
4. Weights (covered bricks)
5. Bone folder

Discretion must be used when flattening creases in the leaves of a book or in maps, documents, or other illustrated materials. Do not attempt to uncrease brittle paper, lest it break along the fold when it is being flattened. If the paper is not brittle, but strong and flexible, the following methods can be used.

A word of caution about these methods. Certain book papers, particularly from older books, have been affected differently by atmospheric and inherent conditions as well as from being handled. Paper is easily stained by water, so the less moisture the better.

These methods are *not* recommended for shiny, clay-coated, calendered paper, which becomes tacky and cockles when moist, or for pages with color illustrations, which may wash out.

Carefully unfold the paper. Place a piece of clean scrap board *under* the fold line and gently but firmly rub down through a waste sheet with a bone folder. If the crease is not reduced or removed, then the following methods can be used with caution.

Unfold the crease and place a piece of blotter under it. With a moistened cotton swab (squeezed tightly to remove any wetness), "paint" along the fold line. Put another blotter on top of the crease and keep under light pressure until dry.

A third method is to "mist" several pieces of blotter with clear water, using a plant mister or a well cleaned spray bottle of the kind ordinarily filled with window cleaning compounds. Place a misted piece of blotter on each side of the crease using waxed paper between the blotters and the adjoining pages so that moisture will not migrate. Place under a light weight until dry.

SEPARATING UNCUT PAGES

Materials and Tools:
1. 3″ × 5″ index cards
2. Bristol scrap
3. Kitchen knife

Pamphlets, journals, and books sometimes have pages left unopened at the head or foredge. These pages should be separated before the materials are shelved; *rare books* are the exception.

Insert an index card, a piece of bristol, or a kitchen knife between the unopened pages. Working outward against the fold (and away from yourself), slit the pages by moving the card, bristol, or knife in a circular pattern. Continue forward, repeating the motion until the entire length is slit.

REMOVING BOOKPLATES

Materials and Tools:
1. Blotter
2. Mylar and waxed paper
3. Photographic trays
4. Weight (covered brick)
5. Micro-Spatula

Where the covers of a book, in need of rebinding, will be discarded, it is easy to remove a bookplate or label that is affixed to the boardsheet.

After carefully detaching the covers from the book block, fill a photographic tray—or similar pan that is larger than the cover—with one-half inch to one inch of warm water. Immerse the cover, bookplate down, to soak for half an hour, then gently lift the loosened bookplate with a bone folder. If the bookplate is still firmly attached, allow it to soak longer, replacing the water if it has cooled.

When the bookplate is off, turn it over in the water and gently rub the underside to remove the remaining adhesive. Place the bookplate between two pieces of clean blotter, with waxed paper next to the adhesive side, and leave it to dry under a light weight for one to two hours.

If the book is not to be rebound and the bookplate is attached to a page of the book, it should be removed by a method that is not difficult, but requires time and patience. First place a piece of waxed paper as a moisture barrier underneath the page. Then cut a piece of blotter the exact size of the bookplate; dampen it and place it directly over the bookplate. Cover it with waxed paper and a light weight. Check every 15 minutes to determine how rapidly the moisture is penetrating the bookplate and loosening the adhesive. Carefully remove the bookplate as soon as the moisture has freed it from the page. Remove the waxed paper and place a piece of blotter on either side of the page from which the bookplate was removed so that moisture will not migrate to adjacent pages. Weight the book under light pressure until it is thoroughly dry.

Residual adhesive on the bookplate can be soaked off in a tray of warm water. Press the bookplate between waxed paper and two blotters, and top with a weight.

MENDING AND REPAIRING TORN PAGES

Repairing cuts and tears in pages is very time-consuming, especially when done in the traditional way, using wheat paste and mending tissue. Paste introduces moisture into the paper and therefore requires a long drying period. The drying period can be cut down considerably by repeated blotting with waste paper to absorb most of the moisture and also by using a mixture of PVA and methyl cellulose instead of paste. This mixture is *not* as reversible as wheat paste.

Alternatives for making quick repairs on replaceable materials are *heat-set tissue* and *pressure-sensitive tapes*, such as Filmoplast® and Ademco®   Both of these are well suited as they are reversible and will not become brittle and leave stains and/or residue. Heat-set tissue, Filmoplast, and Ademco each cost more than twenty times as much as mending tissue. This fact is often not considered when mending tissue repairs are overruled because they are time consuming. Besides being the soundest method of repair, mending with tissue and paste or mixture may prove to be economical as well, once a certain degree of skill is acquired.

Materials:
1. Lens tissue or Japanese tissue (Barcham Green "L" or Tengujo)
2. Waxed paper
3. Waste paper
4. Adhesive: Wheat paste or *mixture* (PVA 40% and methyl cellulose 60%)
5. Scrap pieces of dark colored paper
6. Polyester film scraps

Tools:
1. Small watercolor brush
2. Paste bowl
3. Water bowl
4. Bone folder
5. Tweezers
6. Weight
7. Q-tips

Tears

There are two basic types of tears, the *straight tear*, which follows the direction of the grain and the *curved, feathered tear*, which runs perpendicular to the grain.

The straight tear is characterized by the absence of protruding fibers from the edges of the tear. This type of tear is easily repaired with straight, torn strips of tissue.

The curved, feathered tear, due to cross-grain resistance, usually has ragged edges. This type of tear will cause many fibers to protrude from the edges. The tissue used to repair this type of tear, must be *torn* to a shape that approximately follows the curves of the tear.

STRAIGHT TEARS

1. Place a piece of waxed paper neatly under the tear.

2. Tear a piece of tissue about half an inch wide by half an inch longer than the tear.

3. Coat the tissue with adhesive (wheat paste or a mixture of 40% PVA and 60% methyl cellulose) and place it over the tear, stretching the tissue as little as possible. Allow a small amount of the tissue—perhaps one quarter inch—to extend beyond the edge of the paper. This will be trimmed flush with the edge of the page when the repair is done.

Note: If the paper seems particularly weak or tends to pull away from the mending tissue, put tissue on both sides of the page. In this case the second piece of tissue should be slightly larger than the first one.

4. With waxed paper on each side of the page, rub down to set the tissue and to squeeze out excess adhesive.

5. Replace the pieces of waxed paper with waste paper and continue to rub. Move the waste paper once or twice to absorb as much moisture as possible.

6. Finally, sandwich the mended tear between waxed paper and let the adhesive dry under a weight (one to two hours).

CURVED FEATHERED TEARS

Repair #1. There are three types of repair that can be effectively used to repair curved feathered tears. If enough fibers protrude from the edges in a *feathered tear*, Repair #1, the simplest type of repair, can be used.

1. Place a piece of waste paper underneath the tear. Gently lift up the top layer of the tear so that you can clearly see the exposed fibers on both edges (see Figure 34).

2. Using a small watercolor brush, "paint" a thin coat of adhesive over the exposed fibers along both edges of the tear (see Figure 35).

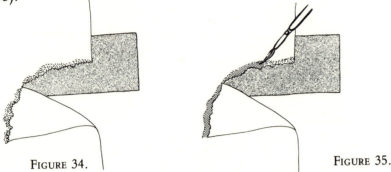

FIGURE 34.   FIGURE 35.

3. Discard the waste paper and replace with a piece of clean waxed paper. Set the edges of the tear back together (see Figure 36).

4. Rub down well with a bone folder through a piece of clean waxed paper. Replace the two pieces of waxed paper with waste paper and continue to rub. Move the waste paper once or twice to absorb as much moisture as possible. Finally, sandwich the mended tear between clean waxed paper and let dry under a weight for one to two hours.

   Note: If there is not enough fiber exposure at the beginning of the tear (near the edge of the page), the tear may not hold together well enough when dry. In that event, a small piece of torn mending tissue can be pasted over the part of the tear closest to the page edge and either turned over the edge and pasted to the other side or trimmed flush (see Figure 37).

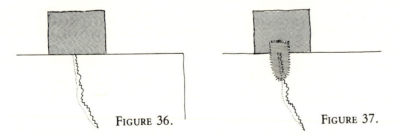

FIGURE 36.   FIGURE 37.

Repair #2. When there are not enough fibers protruding from the edges of the tear Repair #2 can be used.

1. Lift one part of the tear and place a piece of dark colored paper between the two parts so that the outline of the tear is clear (see Figure 38).

2. Place a piece of polyester film which is larger than the area of the tear, on top (see Figure 39).

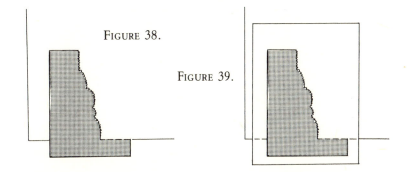

Figure 38.

Figure 39.

3. Roughly cut a piece of mending tissue large enough to accommodate the shape of the tear *plus* 1″. With a small watercolor brush or a Q-tip® dampened in water (but not dripping), "paint" a wet line on the tissue one-eighth to one-quarter inch away from the tear *following its shape* all around. (see Figure 40).

4. Remove the mending tissue from the page and gently pull excess tissue away from the outlined shape. (see Figure 41).

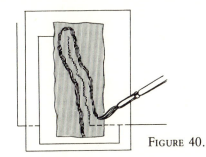 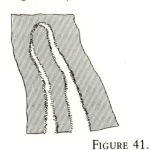

Figure 40.   Figure 41.

5. Turn the tissue over and apply an even thin coat of adhesive. (see Figure 42).

6. Place the tissue over the tear, pasted surface down. (see Figure 43). Proceed as described in Step 4 of the preceding section, page 56.

 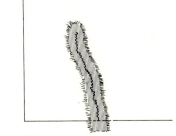

Figure 42.   Figure 43.

Repair #3. The following method combines the *repairs* #1 and #2, and can be used as an *option* for either one.

1. Place a piece of clean waste paper underneath the tear. Rough-cut a piece of mending tissue large enough to accommodate the shape of the tear plus approximately one inch.

2. Lift the top, or upper layer. Using a small watercolor brush, paint a quarter-inch border of adhesive along both edges of the tear (see Figure 44).

3. Place the mending tissue between the two pasted edges of the tear. The mending tissue will adhere to the pasted border of the lower part of the tear (see Figure 45).

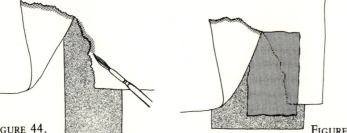

FIGURE 44.   FIGURE 45.

4. Carefully set the edge of the upper layer of the tear down. This edge will adhere to the mending tissue underneath. A small section of the tissue is now adhering to one side of the tear on each side of the leaf (see Figure 46).

5. Rub down well through clean waxed paper and then through waste paper to absorb moisture. Let the repair dry between clean waxed paper under a weight.

6. When the repair has dried completely, gently remove the mending tissue which is not adhered by tearing it away from the pasted-down part (see Figure 47). A pair of tweezers is very handy for this task. Turn the leaf over and repeat the procedure on the other side.

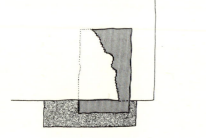

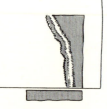

FIGURE 46.   FIGURE 47.

7. While tearing the excess tissue away, some of the tissue fibers may lift up. Apply some paste to the edge of a scrap of polyester film and slide it underneath the lifted up fibers to transfer the paste. Remove the scrap and rub down well through waxed paper.

HINGING, TIPPING AND GUARDING

Hinging and tipping are two methods of attaching loose items to books. These procedures are appropriate for detached plates, errata slips, letters, and up to one loose signature. It is not a good practice to try to hinge or tip-in a large number of loose pages as this will cause further problems. As a general rule, hinging is a better method than tipping. Since a hinge allows the item to swing freely, there is far less strain on the item itself and on the page to which it is attached. When the folded edge of a signature is weak or partly split, a guarding strip is pasted around the damaged fold to strengthen it. A flyleaf, frontispiece, or title page which has separated from the text block should be guarded into a signature and re-attached. This repair is often required before the book can be re-backed.

Materials:
1. Japanese paper (Sekishu)
2. Adhesive: (Wheat paste or mixture)
3. Waxed paper
4. Waste paper (newsprint or old telephone book)

Tools:
1. Scissors
2. Paste brush
3. Paste bowl
4. Bone folder
5. Weights (wrapped bricks)
6. Small weight (jar filled with pennies or lead shot)
7. Pressing boards

Note: Mixture can be substituted for wheat paste. Mixture dries faster, but it is not as easily reversible.

Hinging Single Leaves

1. Cut a hinging strip of Sekishu paper five-eighths inch wide by approximately half an inch longer than the height of the leaf. Hinging strips should always be cut with the grain running in the same direction as that of the item to be hinged. Cut waste paper strips about three inches wide by several inches longer than the height of the leaf.

2. Lay a hinge strip on a piece of waste paper and mask half of it lengthwise with another piece of waste paper. Hold the top piece down firmly. Take a small amount of adhesive on the brush and apply it to the exposed area of the guarding strip with several short brush strokes, away from the waste paper (see Figure 48).

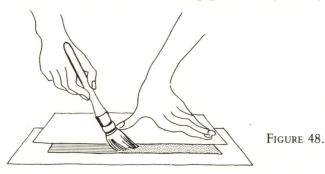

FIGURE 48.

3. Carefully pick up the hinge strip with both hands and set it down on a clean piece of waste paper. Place the leaf to be hinged on the adhesive-covered part of the hinging strip. The strip should extend a little beyond the top and bottom of the leaf. Rub firmly with a bone folder through a piece of clean waste paper (see Figure 49).

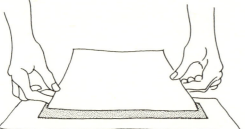

FIGURE 49.

Turn the leaf over and rub again through waste paper to absorb as much moisture as possible. This will shorten drying time and help avoid wrinkling of the leaf. (see Figure 50).

4. Place the leaf in between two strips of clean waste paper and two pressing boards weighted down with a brick. Allow to dry for one to two hours.

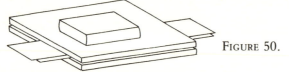

FIGURE 50.

5. Trim the hinge strip to the height of the leaf. (see Figure 51).

FIGURE 51.

6. Fold the unadhered part of the hinge strip back on itself and crease with a bone folder. (see Figure 52).

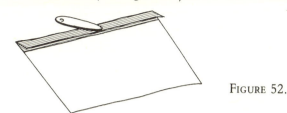

FIGURE 52.

7. Insert clean pieces of waxed paper and waste paper. The waxed paper should be next to the leaf and the waste paper next to the hinge. Apply adhesive to the hinge (see Figure 53). Remove and discard the waste paper.

FIGURE 53.

The following steps describe three different methods of hinging loose materials; the item and its required placement determine the method that should be used.

8a. Position the leaf (errata sheet, letter, plate or map) on the cover or page it will be hinged to. If the leaf is *smaller than the page*, it should be centered; however, if it is the same size, all edges will need to be carefully lined up. In either case, press the pasted hinge down firmly and rub with a bone folder through clean waste paper. Place strips of waxed paper on each side of the adjacent leaves to keep moisture from spreading. Close the book and allow the adhesive to dry completely before removing the waxed paper (see Figure 54).

Note: When hinging or tipping loose materials into a book, the opened book should be supported to provide one horizontal surface. Wooden pressing boards or scrap cardboard can be used to raise and support the open book.

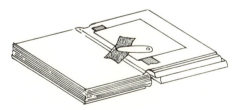

FIGURE 54.

FIGURE 55.

8b. Hinge in a single leaf by inserting a strip of bristol or a flat ruler between the adhesive-coated hinge and the leaf of the book. With the help of the bristol or ruler you can carefully push the leaf all the way back into the gutter margin. To protect adjacent pages in the book from moisture, insert waxed paper strips. As you remove the bristol, close the book and let the adhesive dry (see Figure 55).

8c. Apply adhesive to the inside of the hinge strip and hinge a single leaf (pages from the text or a plate) around a signature (see Figure 56). Rub with a bone folder through clean waste paper. Change the waste paper once or twice to absorb as much moisture as possible.

FIGURE 56.

Tipping

Tipping is the common method of attaching errata slips, detached plates, letters, and single leaves, but although it may be strong at the point of contact, the stress put on adjoining pages does not always recommend it, particularly if the paper to which the item is being attached is weak or brittle.

1. Set the item which is to be attached face down on a piece of clean scrap paper, then put another piece of clean scrap paper on top of the item approximately one-eighth inch away from the edge to be tipped.

2. Brush adhesive along the exposed edge, always brushing from the center outward.

3. Remove the pieces of scrap paper and set the item into place in the book.

4. When the item is in place, rub down and put waxed paper on either side of the item to keep moisture from spreading.

5. Close the book and allow the adhesive to dry completley before removing the waxed paper.

Guarding Single Leaves into a Signature

Original leaves that have become detached such as flyleaves, frontispiece, title page and leaves from the first and last signature or copied replacements of lost leaves can be guarded into a signature.

1. Cut guarding strips of Sekishu paper half an inch wide by half an inch longer than the height of the leaves to be guarded. Guarding strips should *always* be cut with the grain running the length of the fold. (See page 34 on cutting narrow strips.)

   Note: Cutting the guards slightly longer than the height of the leaves or signatures is recommended for several reasons. After adhesive has been applied, the outer ends of the strip may adhere to your fingers when the strip is moved to a clean piece of waste paper. As a consequence the strip may not have enough adhesive to adhere firmly at the top and bottom of the leaf or signature. In addition, a little overhang assures better adhesion all along, and the work can proceed faster if guarding strips do not have to be placed in exact position. Trimming off the extensions later on is not really an added task; even if the strips are cut to the exact height of the leaves or signatures, they are likely to expand slightly after adhesive has been applied and will therefore need trimming in any case.

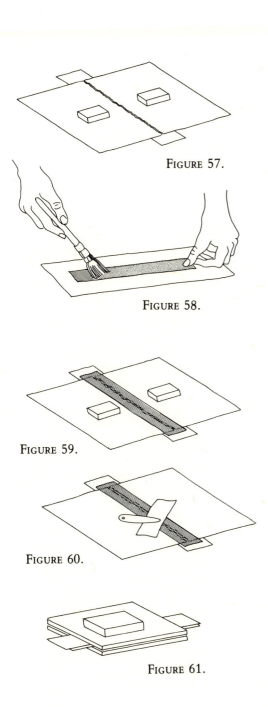

FIGURE 57.

FIGURE 58.

FIGURE 59.

FIGURE 60.

FIGURE 61.

2. Position the two leaves which will become the center of the signature on a piece of waste paper and hold them in place with small weights (see Figure 57). The two inner pages should be side by side, facing you.

3. Lay a guarding strip horizontally on a piece of waste paper (see Figure 58). Take a small amount of adhesive on the brush and, holding the strip in place with your left hand, apply the adhesive from left to right with repeated long brush strokes going in the same direction.

   Note: When a guarding strip is picked up after adhesive has been applied to it, it is moist and will stretch if pulled taut. To avoid this, hold the strip with a little slack. Should a strip be stretched now it will shrink while it is drying, causing the pages to wrinkle.

4. Carefully pick up the guarding strip with both hands and position it over the inner edges of the two leaves. The strip should extend a little beyond the top and bottom of the signature (see Figure 59).

5. Using a bone folder, rub the guarding strip down firmly through the waste paper (see Figure 60). Move or change the waste paper once or twice to absorb as much moisture as possible.

6. Place the guarded leaves between two pieces of waste paper and two pressing boards weighted with a brick. Let the adhesive dry for one to two hours (see Figure 61).

7. Trim the guarding strip to the height of the leaves (see Figure 62).

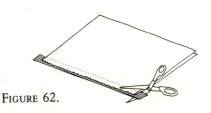

FIGURE 62.

8. Take the next pair of leaves and proceed as described above. When all the leaves are guarded into sheets, dried, and trimmed, they can be folded and inserted in place, making sure that the order is correct (see Figure 63).

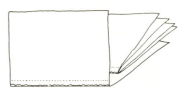

FIGURE 63.

Note: Because of the thickness of the guarding paper the signature may extend slightly at the fore-edge after being sewn in. This extension can be trimmed off with a scalpel, but it is not advised if the fore-edge is deckled or decorated. An alternative method is to trim the leaves slightly at the inner margin before guarding. How much is trimmed depends on the weight of the guarding paper and the number of leaves in the signature. This trimming method should not be attempted by an inexperienced worker.

INSERTING SIGNATURES INTO THE TEXT

If a signature has to be inserted into a bound book it *cannot* be sewn in. Use the following method.

1. Cut a strip of Okawara paper three quarters inch wide and the height of the signature. Fold it in half lengthwise and sew the signature into the strip. The sewing method is the same as is described for the single signature pamphlet binding, page 122. (Tie the loose ends of the sewing thread together with a square knot.)

2. Lay the signature down flat onto the waste paper with *both* flaps of the Okawara paper hinge facing you. Insert clean pieces of waste paper between the flaps and signature. Apply mixture to the Okawara paper strip.

3. Remove the waste paper and discard. Insert a ruler, or a piece of bristol cut larger than the dimension of the paper, into the middle of the signature.

4. Open the book to the place where the signature will be inserted. Holding on to the ruler or bristol, carefully push the signature as far into the gutter margin as possible. Insert clean waxed paper strips on either side of the leaves adjacent to the Okawara paper hinge. Rub with a bone folder and close the book. Apply weight with a brick.

Guarding Signatures with Damaged Folds

Any signature that has damaged folds will need guarding. Often only the outer leaves of these signatures are weak or broken at the fold. In cases where more leaves of a signature are either completely or partially separated, guarding is done from the inside folded leaves of the signature to the outside folded leaves of the signature. Each set of damaged leaves is fitted around the previously guarded leaves.

1. Cut guarding strips of Sekishu paper five-eighths inch wide and half an inch longer than the height of the signature. See Chapter 4, pages 34–35, cutting narrow strips, for cutting more than one guard at a time.

Figure 64.

2. Lay a guarding strip horizontally on a piece of waste paper. Take a small amount of adhesive on the brush and, holding the strip in place with your left hand, apply the adhesive from left to right with repeated long brush strokes going in the same direction (see Figure 64).

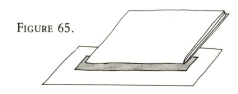

Figure 65.

3. Pick up the guarding strip with both hands, being careful not to stretch it, and put it down on a piece of clean waste paper. Position the folded leaves that are to be guarded around the other inner leaves of the signature and put them down on half of the adhesive-coated guarding strip (see Figure 65). The strip will extend a little beyond the signature at the top and bottom.

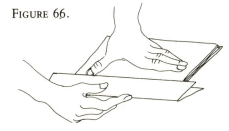

Figure 66.

4. Bring the waste paper around the fold and press down. This action brings the other half of the guard in contact with the signature (see Figure 66).

Figure 67.

5. Remove the signature and rub down with a bone folder through a piece of clean waste paper. Change the waste paper several times to absorb as much moisture as possible (see Figure 67).

6. Repeat the procedure until the signature is complete. Place the complete signature between waxed paper and press under a weight and board until the adhesive is dry.

Figure 68.

7. When dry, trim each pair of guarded leaves with either a scissor or a scalpel. Using the pairs of guarded leaves, assemble the signature (see Figure 68).

BACKING AND LAMINATING PAPER

Backing and laminating can be used only for single sheets or for pages that are detached from a book. These methods are *not* suitable for very fragile, rare, old, or irreplaceable items or for works of art on paper. Items such as these would be candidates for treatment by expeienced conservators.

It is important to remember that backing and laminating operations involve working with wet paper. Although *strong* paper can usually withstand being wet, the characteristics of wet and dry paper differ significantly. Because wet paper will tear, or simply pull apart easily, great care must be taken when handling it.

Printing inks and pencil markings are generally waterproof, but any ink marking should be tested. Using a damp cotton swab, dab an inconspicuous spot such as the dot of an "i" and check to see if the ink runs or comes off. It is advisable to first practice backing and laminating on throwaways. These procedures should never be rushed.

The following instructions presume that the work surface is a matte-finish board. High-gloss surfaces (glass, stainless steel, smooth-finish board) do not work as well, because the pasted-down margins will not peel off when dry; they have to be brushed with water or dabbed with wet cotton before they can be lifted. If you do have to use moisture to release the margins, avoid getting any on the backed page itself. The Japanese paper margins, pasted in direct contact to *matte-finish board*, will peel away from it easily when dry. They do not give while the backed page shrinks as it dries. This tension causes the page to dry taut, without wrinkles.

Materials:
1. Japanese paper (Sekishu)
2. Barcham Green lens tissue
3. Adhesive—(Wheat paste *only*)
4. Polyester web (such as Pellon)
5. Paper towels (unpatterned white—reusable after drying)
6. Blotters

Tools:
1. Two brushes (one for paste, one for water) soft, natural bristles, one and one-half to two inches in diameter
2. Two dishes (one for paste, one for water)
3. Matte-finish board
4. Soaking pan (plastic photographer's tray or glass, stainless steel, or enamel baking pan) larger than the paper to be soaked
5. Mat (utility) knife
6. Metal straightedge

7. Weights (covered bricks)
8. Pressing boards
9. Pink Pearl® eraser or Opaline® bag

Backing Paper

The term *backing* refers to the technique of supporting paper from the back. This method is appropriate for reinforcing worn or fragile pages and pamphlet covers that have no printing on one side. Japanese paper of medium weight, such as Sekishu, can be used since there is no danger of obscuring any text. This paper is easier to handle than the very thin Barcham Green lens tissue used for lamination (see pp. 69, 70) and will peel away from the matte-finish surface easily when it is dry. Always check to see whether the inks or markings on the page are water-soluble; if they dissolve in water they are, and this would *not* be an acceptable treatment.

1. Clean the page if necessary, as described on pages 51, 52.
   Do not attempt to clean delicate paper.

2. Find the grain direction of the page to be backed (see Chapter 5, pp. 42–43); rough-cut a piece of Sekishu paper about two inches longer and wider than the page; be sure that the grain of the Sekishu paper runs in the same direction as that of the page.

3. To give paper support when wet, especially if it already shows signs of tearing, cut a piece of *Polyester-web* (see Supply Sources, pp. 147–148), a thick, non-woven material which provides stable support while the paper is being moved from water to board. Water drains away from the polyester web almost instantly. The web is reusable.

4. Fill a pan with warm water to a depth of about one inch. Place the Polyester web supported leaf that is to be backed into the water to soak for about ten minutes or until it is thoroughly wet.

Figure 69.

5. Carefully lift the polyester web out of the water with the page on it (see Figure 69); set it on a matte-finish board, so that the polyester web is on top and the page, face down, is on the bottom; remove the web and gently work out air bubbles and wrinkles with the water brush. Pat some of the water off the page with a paper towel. Rinse and dry the web for future use.

6. Brush a thin layer of adhesive (wheat paste) evenly over the back of the page, brushing from the center of the page outward. "Paint" a border of paste about two inches wide around the page on the board (see Figure 70 and 71).

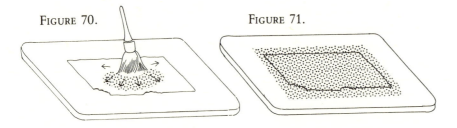

FIGURE 70.   FIGURE 71.

7. Set the piece of dry Sekishu paper down along one short side of the page, holding it in place by pressing it to the adhesive border (see Figure 72).

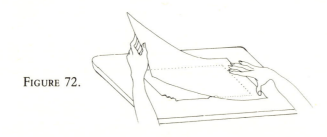

FIGURE 72.

8. Slowly roll the Sekishu paper onto the page, brushing it into place with a soft brush dipped only in water (see Figure 73); brushing from the center of the page outward, work out any air bubbles; finally, brush the outer margins of the Sekishu paper down well onto the border of paste around the page; pat some of the excess water off the Sekishu with a paper towel.

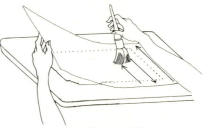

FIGURE 73.

9. Leave the page to dry until the edges of the Sekishu paper begin to lift away from the board. This will usually take 30 minutes to two hours, depending on the humidity. Peel the page away from the board. To keep the page from curling, place it between clean blotters and put it under a board weighted down with bricks. Leave it to dry overnight.

10. Using a mat knife and a metal straightedge, trim away the excess Sekishu. If the page is to be tipped or sewn into a book or pamphlet, leave a three-quarter inch extension of the Sekishu along the gutter margin. Be sure to hold the straightedge down firmly, cutting with a light stroke, several times if necessary.

Laminating Paper

The process of *lamination*, placing a very thin paper or tissue on *both* sides of the page, is used when a leaf is printed on both sides, because paper used for backing is heavier and would obscure the print on one side. Lamination forms a sandwich with the page as the middle layer. Always check to be sure that the inks or markings on the page are not water-soluble, if they are, lamination would *not* be an acceptable treatment.

1. If the page is not too fragile, clean it as described on page 51. Do not attempt to clean delicate paper.

2. Rough-cut two pieces of Barcham Green lens tissue about two inches longer and wider than the page. No need to consider the grain direction in this case; lens tissue is so thin as to have no *obvious* grain.

3. Fill a pan with about an inch of warm water. Set a piece of polyester web, larger than the leaf, into the water. Place the page on top of the web. Allow the paper to soak for about ten minutes or until it is thoroughly wet.

4. Lift the polyester web out of the water with the leaf on it. Set it down on the board with the polyester web on the bottom and the page on top. Gently work out air bubbles and wrinkles with the water brush. Remove some of the excess water from the leaf with a paper towel. (see Figure 74).

5. Brush a thin layer of wheat paste evenly over the surface of the page, working from the center outward; do not be concerned about paste being brushed beyond the edges. (see Figure 75 and 76).

6. Align the Barcham Green lens tissue along one short edge of the page. (see Figure 77).

7. Slowly roll the tissue down onto the page, brushing it into place with the soft brush that has been dipped only in water. Work out all air bubbles from the center of the page outward. Remove excess water from the tissue with a paper towel. (see Figure 78).

FIGURE 74.

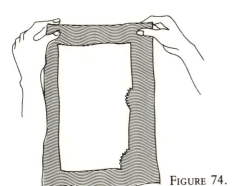

FIGURE 75.

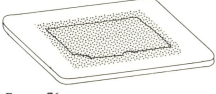

FIGURE 76.

FIGURE 77.   FIGURE 78.

8. "Paint" a border of paste on the margins of the tissue. Lift the page, supported by the polyester web, off the board. Set it down on a clean dry section of board—*tissue side to board*. Gently peel the web off the page and work out air bubbles and wrinkles with the water brush. Rinse and dry the web for future use.

9. Brush a thin layer of wheat paste evenly over the surface of the upturned page and tissue, working from the center outward. (see Figure 79).

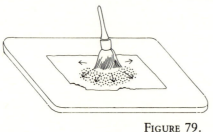

FIGURE 79.

10. Align the edge of the dry Barcham Green lens tissue along one short edge of the paste-covered tissue. (see Figure 80).

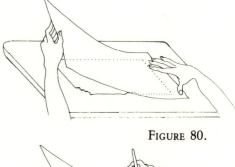

FIGURE 80.

11. Slowly roll the tissue down over the page, brushing it into place with a soft brush dipped only in water; work out all air bubbles from the center outward; remove excess water from the tissue with a paper towel. (see Figure 81).

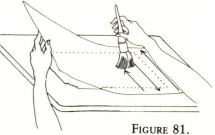

FIGURE 81.

12. With the wet brush, brush over the margins of the tissue, so as to temporarily seal them to the board.

13. Allow the page to dry until the edges of the tissue begin to lift away from the board. This will usually take half an hour to two hours, depending on the humidity. Peel the page away from the board. As the paper may tend to curl, place it between two pieces of clean blotter and put it under a board weighted down with bricks. Allow it to dry.

14. Using a mat knife and a metal straightedge, trim away the excess tissue. If the page is to be tipped or sewn into a book or pamphlet, leave a three-quarter inch extension of the tissue along the gutter margin. Be sure to hold the straightedge down firmly while cutting with a light stroke. Cut several times if necessary.

REPAIRING HARDBOUND CLOTH OR PAPER-COVERED CORNERS

The corners of a binding are particularly vulnerable to damage. Because of hard use and/or abuse, the corner covering materials can become frayed or worn and the binder's board underneath can separate into layers or be crushed. Several simple steps can be undertaken to repair this type of damaged corner. These steps are *not* however, recommended for full leather bindings or bindings that have leather corners.

Materials:
1. Adhesive: 50% PVA and 50% Methyl Cellulose
2. Small squares of waxed paper or polyester film
3. Small squares of binder's board or stiff cardboard (2″ × 2″)
4. Bulldog clips, Boston clamps or small C clamps
5. Newsprint
6. Scissors
7. Bookcloth scraps (various textures and colors)

Tools:
1. Paste container
2. Small paint brush (polyester bristles)
3. Microspatula or bookbinder's knife
4. Bulldog clips, Boston clamps or small C clamps
5. Bone folder

Frayed Cloth or Loose Threads

1. With your fingers, work a small amount of adhesive into the frayed cloth or loose threads and put the threads in place (see Figure 82).

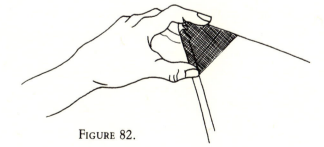

FIGURE 82.

2. Fold a piece of waxed paper around the board and rub it back and forth along the edges and around the corner (see Figure 83). This will consolidate the fibers with the adhesive and help shape the corner.

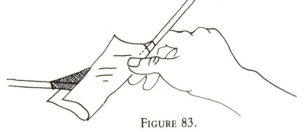

FIGURE 83.

Cloth or Paper Lifted from the Corner

If bookcloth or book-covering paper has become detached from the binder's board at the corner it can easily be put down again. This can be done using a piece of scrap bristol and adhesive.

1. Apply the adhesive to the bristol and slip it (with the adhesive side adjacent to the cloth or paper) between the covering materials and the board (Figure 84).

FIGURE 84.

2. Apply pressure and pull the bristol out, leaving the adhesive transferred to the material. Discard the used bristol.

3. Place the original covering material back in position and rub down, through clean waste paper, with the flat side of a bone folder.

4. Wipe away any adhesive that appears at the edges.

5. With waxed paper wrapped around the edges, carefully shape the corner.

Separated Layers of Binder's Board

1. Apply adhesive to a piece of bristol or a microspatula and transfer it to the area between the split layers of binder's board (Figure 85). Apply additional adhesive where it is necessary.

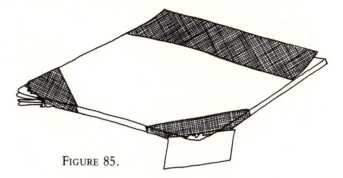

FIGURE 85.

2. Press the layers of board together firmly, wipe off any excess moisture, and reshape the corner.

3. Put a piece of waxed paper or film against the top and bottom surface of the corner and cover the paper with pieces of binder's board.

4. Clamp this "sandwich" together with a C-clamp (or Boston clamp) and leave it until dry (Figure 86).

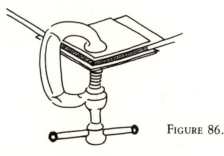

FIGURE 86.

Recovering Corners

If the corner repairs previously described have been made, the corners should be sound and re-covering will not be necessary. The following instructions are included for those books on which corner re-covering may be deemed desirable.

Note: It is preferable to lift the original covering material from the binder's board at the corner before re-covering with new material and then pasting the original covering material back into place. However, if the original covering material is brittle or difficult to lift, the new material may be pasted on top. When the new covering material must be placed over the original, omit steps 1 and 2.

1. Slit and lift the covering material by inserting a knife between the covering material and the board. Lift at least one inch on either side of the corner (see Figure 87).

   Note: The covering materials and paper pastedown (boardsheet) should be lifted as one piece.

FIGURE 87.

2. Hold the knife blade parallel to the board. Push slowly but firmly, with a circular motion to separate the covering material and the pastedown from the board (see Figure 88).

   Note: If the layers of binder's board have been separated, consolidate them as described in the previous section.

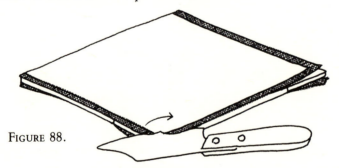

FIGURE 88.

3. Cut a triangle of bookcloth (use paper if the original corner covering was paper) large enough to cover the worn area of the corner with an additional one-half-inch margin on two sides for the turn-ins.

Note: To measure the size of the triangle, place the corner of the board on the re-covering material. One-half-inch margins should extend on either side for the turn-ins. Make a pencil mark at the point to which you have lifted the original covering material and cut the new material at this mark (see Figure 89).If more than one corner is being recovered fold the triangle over at the mark and cut the material into a square. Cut along the fold to get two triangles of equal size (see Figure 90).

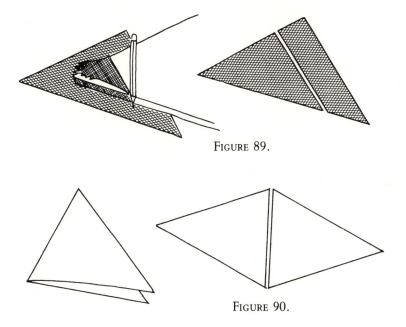

FIGURE 89.

FIGURE 90.

4. Brush adhesive on the back of the triangle.

5. Place the triangle between the board and the old covering material so that the one-half-inch turn-ins extend beyond the board. (see Figure 91).

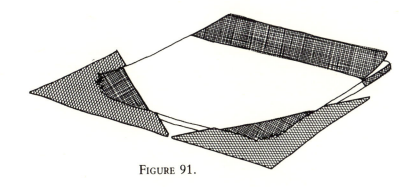

FIGURE 91.

6. Rub the triangle through clean wastepaper with a bone folder; allow the adhesive to dry for a few minutes.

7. Cut off the top angle of the triangle leaving slightly more than one board thickness of material to cover the corner tip of the board later. Trim away the other two angles (see Figure 92).

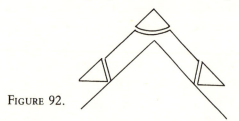

FIGURE 92.

8. Brush additional adhesive on the extending margins (see Figure 93).

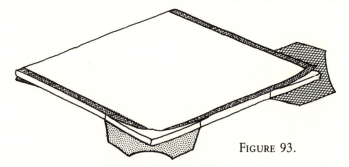

FIGURE 93.

9. Turn in one margin of the triangle and rub down well. A small piece of material will extend beyond the corner (see Figure 94).

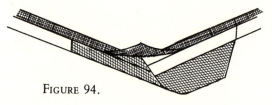

FIGURE 94.

10. Using a fingernail or the tip of a bone folder tuck the overhang into the remaining margin before making the second turn-in (see Figure 95). This step will cover the tip of the board.

FIGURE 95.

11. Turn in the other margin of the triangle. It will slightly overlap the material from the first turn-in. Rub down well through wastepaper.

REBACKING OF CLOTH BINDINGS

If a book is completely separated from its case or has a loose spine, worn out joints, broken hinges, or detached boards, it can be rebacked provided the sewing is still intact and strong. Carefully examine the book by opening several signatures. Locate the sewing and pull the thread gently to test its strength. If the sewing is not sound, rebacking is *not* a practical solution.

More appropriate solutions for books with weak sewing include *preservation enclosures* or *library bindings.* Rare or valuable books, unusual and historically important bindings, as well as most books printed before 1850, should not be rebacked. These materials are better off in preservation enclosures until they can be properly restored or re-bound by a skilled conservator or bookbinder.

Materials:
1. Acid-free paper (60 - 80 lb.)
2. Acid-free bristol
3. Buckram or other book cloth
4. Unbleached Irish linen thread (size 30)
5. Japanese paper (Okawara)
6. Adhesive: 50% PVA and 50% Methyl cellulose
7. Waxed paper
8. Newsprint

For Headbands:
1. Linen cord (3 or 5 cord)
2. Linen or 100% cotton shirting

Tools:
1. Scalpel
2. Steel ruler
3. Scissors
4. Bone folder
5. Paste brush
6. Paste bowl
7. Weights (wrapped bricks)
8. Pressing boards (metal edged) or card cabinet drawer rods or knitting needles
9. Microspatula
10. Kitchen knife
11. Pencil
12. Damp cotton rag

Rebacking with Attached Boards

Cloth bindings that have broken outer joints, but intact inner hinges, can be rebacked using the following method:

1. Remove the original cloth intact from the spine and set it aside for reapplication. Clean the spine of the bookblock, removing all loose super (mull, paper layers, and glue).

2. Using a scalpel, make a cut one-eighth inch in from the spine edge of the board. Turn the book over and repeat this step (see Figure 96). *Be careful not to cut into the inner hinge.*

3. Peel the narrow strips of original cloth off the edge of each board (see Figure 97).

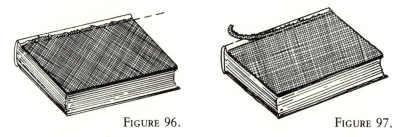

FIGURE 96.   FIGURE 97.

Note: The extensions of the new cloth spine that will be affixed to the front and back boards can either be placed over or underneath the original covering material. When the new cloth will be placed underneath, the original material must first be lifted using a scalpel or microspatula, from the boards. This method is preferable when there is textual information and/or artwork on the original, or if the original material can be lifted easily without tearing.

4. Using a scalpel, slit the bookcloth at the head and tail edges of the board approximately one inch down (see Figure 98).

FIGURE 98.

5. Carefully insert a knife under the trimmed edge of the cloth at a point where it can be lifted easily. Hold the knife parallel to the board and slowly but firmly, push it forward using a circular motion. Lift back the old cloth approximately one inch from the board edge (see Figure 99). The new cloth will be pasted underneath later. Turn the book over and repeat steps four and five on the other side.

FIGURE 99.

6. Cut a piece of acid-free paper to the height of the spine of the bookblock by one-eight inch *less* than three times the width of the spine. Make sure the grain of the paper runs parallel to the spine. Make small creases at the top and bottom to mark the middle (see Figure 100).

FIGURE 100.

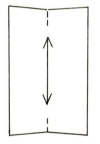

7. Determine the center point of the spine and make a pencil mark at the head and tail.

8. Apply adhesive to the spine (see Figure 101).

9. Center the acid-free paper on the spine by matching the creases with the pencil marks (see Figure 102). Rub well with a bone folder and let the adhesive dry.

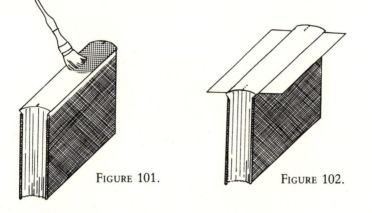

FIGURE 101.   FIGURE 102.

10. Apply adhesive to one flap (flap A) (see Figure 103).

11. Fold the other flap (flap B) over a strip of waxed paper, cut to the same width as the spine, and paste flap A on top of flap B (see Figure 104). Rub down well with a bone folder. Move the wax paper strip back and forth several times to make sure that it does not adhere. Let the adhesive dry.

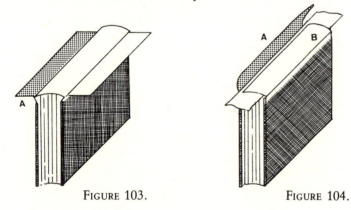

FIGURE 103.   FIGURE 104.

12. Cut a piece of book cloth the height of the spine *plus* one and one-half inches and the width of the spine *plus* two inches. The grain of the cloth must run parallel to the spine (see Figure 105).

13. Cut a piece of bristol the height of the boards by the exact width of the spine. The grain of the bristol must run parallel to both the cloth *and* the spine. Mark the middle of the cloth *and* bristol pieces (see Figure 106).

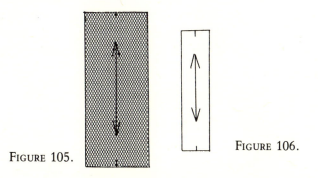

FIGURE 105.

FIGURE 106.

14. Apply adhesive to the bristol strip. Center it on the under side of the cloth (see Figure 107) and rub down. Weigh down with a brick and let the adhesive dry.

FIGURE 107.

15. Using a kitchen knife, slit the tube at the top and bottom, make the cuts three-quarters of an inch deep (see Figure 108).

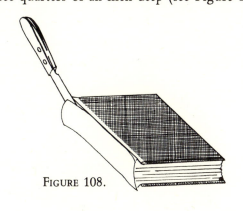

FIGURE 108.

16. Open the book and support the cover with boards. Insert the kitchen knife under the hinge at the edge of the cover. Hold the knife as flat as possible and slowly but firmly, push the knife forward with a circular motion. Lift the board sheet and covering material turn-in as one piece. Free an area about one inch by three-quarters of an inch, or enough to accommodate the turn-in of the new cloth spine (see Figure 109).

Note: If it is too difficult to lift the boardsheet, open the covers of the book and make three-quarters of an inch deep cuts at the top and the bottom of both joints with a pair of scissors, so that the new cloth can be inserted through the slits when the turn-ins are made at a later step (see Figure 110).

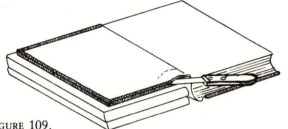

FIGURE 109.

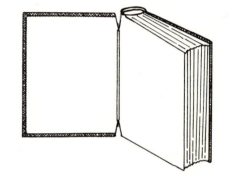

FIGURE 110.

17. Apply adhesive to the bristol and cloth piece. The waxed paper strip should still be in the tube. If it has been removed insert two pieces of waxed paper, one at the top and one at the bottom of the tube to stop the adhesive from seeping between the layers and pasting the tube shut.

18. Align the bristol with the tube and flush with the edges of the boards at head and tail.

19. Affix the extending new cloth to each board underneath the lifted-up original covering material (see Figure 111).

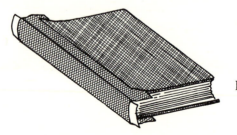

FIGURE 111.

20. Work the new cloth into the joints with a bone folder.

21. Affix the lifted-up covering material with adhesive to the new cloth. Place between two boards and let dry.

    Note: Metal-edged pressing boards or knitting needles may be pressed into the joint grooves. (See page 92 for details.) If the original covering material was not lifted, affix the new cloth with adhesive over it (see Figure 112).

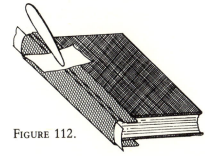

FIGURE 112.

22. Stand the book on a board. Allow the tail to hang over the edge of the board so that the extending cloth does not get crushed (see Figure 113).

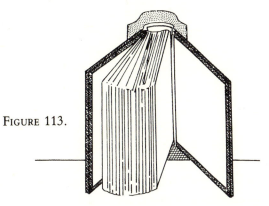

FIGURE 113.

23. Apply adhesive to the extending cloth at the head (see Figure 114).

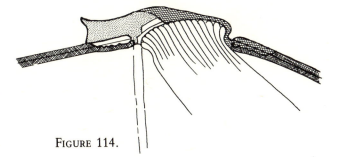

FIGURE 114.

24. Turn in the cloth, slide it through the slits previously made in the tube and under the lifted boardsheet.

25. Apply adhesive under the lifted portion of the boardsheet and rub down well with the bone folder.

26. Repeat steps 22, 23 and 24 at the tail.

    Note: If the boardsheet was not lifted, turn the cloth, slide it through the slits in the tube and cut apart sections of the joints (see Figure 115). Affix the cloth over the boardsheet.

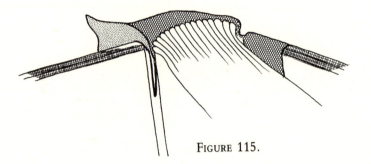

FIGURE 115.

27. Clean off all loose glue and paper lining from the *original* spine. Trim the frayed edges with a scalpel or cutter.

28. Apply adhesive and affix the original spine to the new cloth making sure the title is right side up. Rub the original spine through wastepaper, with a bone folder and allow the adhesive to dry.

Rebacking with Detached Boards

Books that have completely detached covers or cases can be rebacked to replace deteriorated spines and broken hinges. Check headbands and flyleaves as they will often require reattachment before proceeding.

Separate the boards and spine into three *separate* components. This is important as the original cloth hinges may be weak and when reinforced will not fit back over the bookblock.

(The materials list is the same for both *attached* and detached boards, see p. 71).

1. Lay the detached boards and spine aside for reapplication at a later step. Examine the text block to see that the sewing is sound. If it is not sound, rebacking is *not* a practical solution.

2. Clean the spine of all loose super (mull), paper layers and glue.

Note: If the headbands are loose, frayed or broken, remove them and make new ones following steps 3–6. Omit these steps if the book has sound headbands. Pasted-on headbands are not necessary to the structure of the book and can be left off.

3. Take a piece of linen cord a little longer than twice the width of the spine. Coat it with adhesive and let it dry (see Figure 116).

FIGURE 116.

4. Cut a piece of linen or cotton shirting as wide as the linen cord is long, by one and one-half inches (see Figure 117).

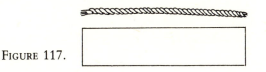

FIGURE 117.

5. Apply adhesive to the cloth and set the stiffened piece of cord on it, above the middle of the cloth (see Figure 118).

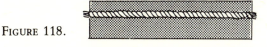

FIGURE 118.

6. Fold the narrow part of the cloth over the cord. Press down and work a bone folder along the covered cord (see Figure 119). Let the adhesive dry. This will be the headband.

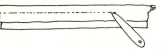

FIGURE 119.

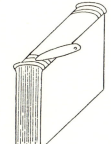

FIGURE 120.

7. From the headband cut two pieces, each the exact width of the spine. Paste them to the head and tail of the book so that the covered linen cord fits snugly over the head and tail. Rub them down well with a bone folder (see Figure 120).

Note: A finishing or lying press will provide good support when working on the spine of a book. If neither is available, hold the book firmly between your knees when working with the bone folder.

Missing or detached flyleaves can be replaced with new ones made of acid-free paper. Omit steps 8–11 if the flyleaves are intact, or are being repaired as described on pages 92–94 of this chapter.

8. Cut a piece of acid-free paper to the height of the pages and wide enough to wrap around the textblock *plus* a little extra (about one inch).

9. Apply adhesive to the spine of the bookblock.

10. Carefully "paint" a thin line of adhesive (about one-eighth-inch wide) along the front and back shoulders of the bookblock (see Figure 121).

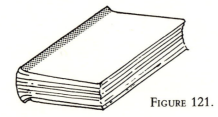

FIGURE 121.

11. Place the bookblock on the righthand portion of the acid-free paper so that the paper extends slightly beyond the fore-edge about one-quarter of an inch (see Figure 122).

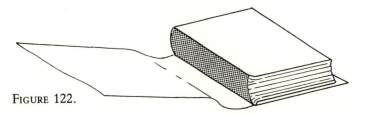

FIGURE 122.

12. Bring the acid-free paper up and around the spine and rub it down well (see Figure 123). Draw the bone folder along the shoulders of the bookblock through a piece of wastepaper, firmly pressing against the shoulder.

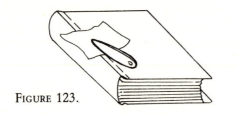

FIGURE 123.

13. Bend the acid-free paper over the fore-edge (see Figure 124).

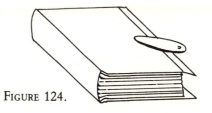

Figure 124.

14. Slip a piece of scrap board underneath the acid-free paper. Using a steel ruler and a scalpel cut the acid-free paper, along the bend, to the page size (see Figure 125).

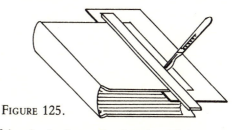

Figure 125.

15. Cut a piece of book cloth to the height of the spine. Cut the width measurement to that of the spine *plus* two inches.

16. Affix the bookcloth to the spine of the bookblock with adhesive. One inch of book cloth should extend on either side. Rub down well with a bone folder (see Figure 126). Let the adhesive dry.

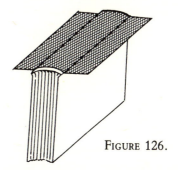

Figure 126.

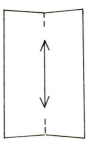

Figure 127.

17. Cut a piece of acid-free paper to the height of the spine of the bookblock by one-eighth inch *less* than three times the width of the spine. The grain of the paper must run parallel to the spine. Make small creases at top and bottom to mark the middle (see Figure 127).

18. Determine the center of the spine and make a pencil mark at the head and tail.

19. Apply adhesive to the spine (see Figure 128A).

20. Center the acid-free paper on the spine by matching the creases with the pencil marks (see Figure 128B). Rub the paper with a bone folder. Let the adhesive dry.

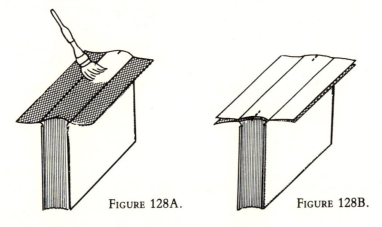

FIGURE 128A.   FIGURE 128B.

21. Apply adhesive to flap A (see Figure 129).

22. Fold flap B over a strip of waxed paper and paste flap A on top of flap B (see Figure 130). Rub down well with a bone folder. Move the waxed paper strip back and forth several times to make sure that it does not adhere. Let the adhesive dry.

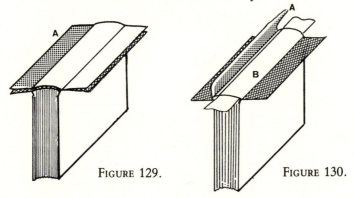

FIGURE 129.   FIGURE 130.

23. First, cut a piece of bristol to the height of the boards by the exact width of the spine. Then, cut a piece of book cloth one and one-half inches longer than the bristol strip by two inches wider than the bristol strip.

24. Apply adhesive to the bristol. Center and then carefully affix it to the book cloth. Place under weights and let the adhesive dry for ten minutes.

25. To prepare the boards for reapplication, make a cut with a scalpel along the spine, one-eighth inch in from the spine edge of the board (see Figure 131).

26. Peel the narrow strip of the original cloth off the edge of the board (see Figure 132).

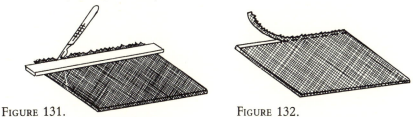

FIGURE 131.   FIGURE 132.

Note: The extensions of the new cloth spine that will be affixed to the front and back boards can either be placed over or underneath the original covering material. When the new cloth will be placed underneath, the original material must first be lifted from the boards. This method is preferable particularly where there is textual information and/or art work on the original, or if the original material can be lifted easily without tearing.

27. Using a scalpel, slit the bookcloth at the edge of the board approximately one inch down (see Figure 133).

28. Carefully insert a knife under the trimmed edge of the cloth at a point where it can be lifted easily. Hold the knife parallel to the board and slowly but firmly, push it forward using a circular motion. Lift the old cloth back, approximately one inch from the board edge. The new cloth will be pasted underneath the original cloth later (see Figure 134).

FIGURE 133.   FIGURE 134.

29. Sandwich the bookblock between the boards, making sure the front and back boards are in the right place. Use the board sheets as guides to even the square on all sides. Then lay the book down on the table with the spine clear of the table's edge. Place a weight on the book to hold it securely.

30. Apply adhesive to the cloth area around the bristol spine strip. *Do not get any adhesive on the bristol at this time* (see Figure 135).

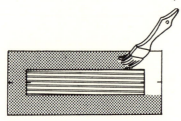

FIGURE 135.

31. Bend the bristol around the spine of the book, making sure that it is centered *and* aligned with the boards at head and tail.

32. When the bristol is in position, grasp the spine firmly and affix the extending cloth with adhesive either underneath or on top of the original bookcloth, first on one side then on the other (see Figure 136A). Rub down with a bone folder through wastepaper (see Figure 136B).

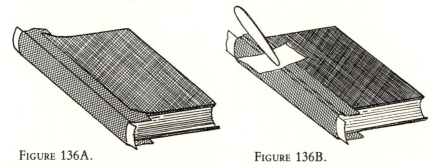

FIGURE 136A.   FIGURE 136B.

33. Take the bookblock out of the case. Apply adhesive to the extending cloth and turn it in at head and tail. Work the cloth into the joints with a bone folder and rub them down well (see Figure 137).

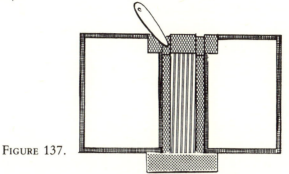

Figure 137.

34. Fit the case around the book again, making sure that the cover and bookblock are *both* right side up and aligned.

35. Open the front cover. Insert strips of waxed paper and wastepaper between the flyleaf and the bookcloth hinge. The waxed paper must be next to the flyleaf and the wastepaper next to the hinge (see Figure 138).

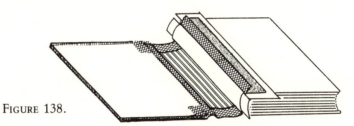

Figure 138.

36. Apply adhesive to the bookcloth hinge, the spine, and the bristol strip, for good adhesion. *Discard the wastepaper strip.*

37. Holding the bookblock firmly, close the cover and rub the spine down well, first with your hand, and then with a bone folder through wastepaper (see Figure 139).

Figure 139.

38. Affix the original cloth with adhesive if it has been lifted. Lay a clean strip of wastepaper over the joint and draw the bone folder along it several times. *Do not open the cover until dry.*

39. Turn the book over. Affix the back bookcloth hinge and the original cloth covering as described above for the front hinge. Work in the joint and rub well.

40. Place the book between two metal-edged boards and weigh down with a brick. The metal edges should fit into the joint grooves (see Figure 140A). If metal-edged boards are not available, knitting needles, card catalogue drawer rods or some similar rods may be pressed into the grooves. A board on each side and weights will hold them in place (see Figure 140B).

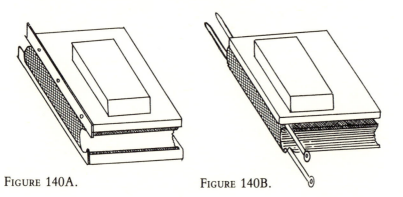

FIGURE 140A.   FIGURE 140B.

Note: The original spine can be pasted on top of the new cloth spine. All loose paper lining and glue should be cleaned off the original spine, and frayed edges trimmed with a scalpel or cutter.

41. Apply adhesive and affix the original spine to the new cloth, *making sure the title is right side up.* Rub down the original spine with a bone folder through wastepaper and leave to dry.

Sewing on End Signatures

Sometimes the flyleaves, frontispiece, title page or the first or last text pages have separated from the bookblock. Torn, fragile or partly detached pages should be removed from the bookblock. They can be *mended, backed* or *laminated* and *guarded* into a signature (see Chapter 6).

It is particularly important to prepare end signatures properly since they have to withstand a great deal of strain.

1. Guard the damaged pages into a signature following procedures in Chapter 6.

2. Lay the detached boards and spine aside for reapplication at a later step.

3. Clean the spine of all loose super (mull), paper layers and glue.

4. For instructions on preparing the spine, turn to pp. 87–88, steps 15–22 (this Chapter). After step 22, continue from step 5 below.

5. Cut two strips of Okawara paper to a one-half-inch width by the height of the bookblock.

6. Fold the strips in half lengthwise.

7. Insert a piece of wastepaper in the fold of the Okawara paper strips and apply adhesive to one-half of the outside of each strip. Discard the wastepaper.

8. Affix the adhesive-coated side of the Okawara paper strip along the spine side of the bookblock so that the fold is next to the spine. Rub down with a bone folder and let it dry for ten minutes (see Figure 141).

Note: If pages are detached at the other end, turn the bookblock over and using the second strip, repeat steps six and seven.

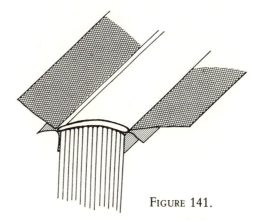

FIGURE 141.

9. Insert strips of waxed paper and wastepaper. The waxed paper must be next to the book and the wastepaper next to the free-swinging portion of the Okawara paper hinge. Apply adhesive to the hinge (see Figure 142).

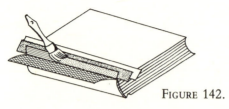

FIGURE 142.

10. Discard the wastepaper. Align the repaired signature with the edges of the text block and affix it to the adhesive-coated Okawara paper hinge. Rub down through wastepaper with a bone folder. If necessary, repeat the process on the other side (see Figure 143).

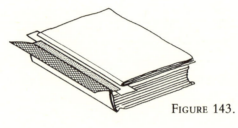

FIGURE 143.

11. Thread a needle with linen thread two and one-half times the height of the bookblock. Open the signature to its middle. Mark and pierce five holes through both the signature and the cloth hinge at the same time.

12. Start the sewing from the outside, entering through the middle hole (see Figure 144). Tie the two loose ends of the sewing thread together with a square knot. If necessary, repeat the process on the other side.

13. For instructions on reattaching the cover boards, turn to pages 88–92 (this Chapter), and follow steps 23–41.

FIGURE 144.

Wrappers, folders, slipcases, and boxes—referred to as enclosures—can be either a temporary or a permanent means of protecting books and other materials from light, dust, and excessive or rough handling. Enclosures are safe, economical, relatively simple and fast to make; they lend support to fragile materials; and they keep components securely in one place.

To achieve their protective purpose, enclosures must be made of durable, archival-quality materials. Although enclosures restrict access, a label pasted to the outside of an enclosure can facilitate identification of the item inside and its condition.

Today there are a vast number of books (not necessarily rare) in need of preservation treatment. Currently the number of skilled workers available to work with deteriorating library materials is limited. Enclosures are economical, simple, and sensible and as such are the best option. Many books can be put into enclosures for the price of having one book restored. What is more, many conservators and librarians believe that, as a means of retarding deterioration, without physically altering the material, a lasting enclosure is preferable.

This chapter describes the preparation of a variety of enclosures. A prerequisite for making these enclosures is a good paper cutter. Without one, the procedures can be laborious and inefficient. Institutions that have no facilities for producing large quantities of enclosures for books which require individual and immediate attention, should consider *wrappers* and *phase-boxes* purchased from commercial suppliers. These may prove more economical especially if they can be purchased in large quantity.

STORAGE WRAPPER

Materials that are put into storage for an indefinite time should be wrapped to protect them. It is a good idea to establish a storage system that makes each item readily accessible and provides for reuse of the wrapper enclosing it. The storage wrapper is also useful in the preparation for shipment of valuable or fragile items. Additional protection is provided by enclosing the wrapper in plastic bubble wrap. For shipped items that are to be returned, a note should be included, requesting that the items be rewrapped in the same materials.

Materials:
1. Plastic bubble wrap (only for shipping)
2. Acid-free tissue paper
3. Acid-free wrapping paper

Tools:
1. Bone folder
2. Paper cutter
3. Scissors

1. Wrap the book in two sheets of acid-free tissue paper and turn the package over to keep the wrapping secure. Adhesive tape is *not* needed and not recommended (Figure 145 and 146).

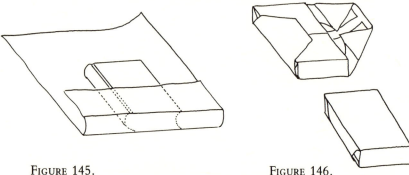

FIGURE 145.   FIGURE 146.

2. Cut a piece of acid-free wrapping paper to twice the height of the book and two and a half times its width *plus* two thicknesses. This outer wrapper will keep the package secure, provide some cushioning, and act as a surface on which to write the title, call number, and other information.

   Note: The dimensions of the wrapping paper do not have to be exact. It is not necessary to tailor each piece of paper to each individual book, especially when many books are being wrapped. To do the job efficiently and quickly, organize books or other items roughly by size and pre-cut the wrapping paper to approximate sizes.

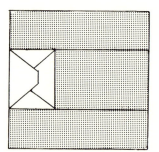

FIGURE 147.

3. Center the tissue wrapped book on the piece of wrapping paper, flush with one edge (Figure 147).

4. Place one hand firmly on the book. With your other hand fold up the paper at head and tail and crease it against the edges of the book.

5. Remove the book and sharpen the creases, using a bone folder, across the entire piece of wrapping paper (see Figure 148).

FIGURE 148.

6. Place the wrapped book on the *folded* piece of wrapping paper.

7. First bring the lefthand extending portion of the paper over, align it with the fore-edge, hold it firmly in place and crease it around the spine. Then bring the righthand extending portion over and crease around the fore-edge (see Figure 149).

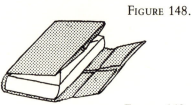

FIGURE 149.

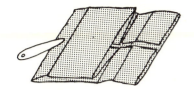

FIGURE 150.

8. Remove the book and sharpen the creases with a bone folder (see Figure 150).

9. Place the wrapped book back on the folded paper. Fold both corners of the righthand flaps at an angle (Figure 151).

10. Tuck the flap with the folded corners *into* the lefthand flap (see Figure 152).

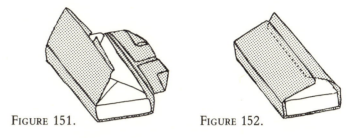

FIGURE 151.   FIGURE 152.

SELF-CLOSING WRAPPER

Originally designed as a temporary holding device, wrappers have proved effective and durable. Next to the *storage wrapper*, the *self-closing wrapper* is the most economical enclosure to make. Self-closing wrappers can be used for materials designated for rebinding or restoring at a later date; or can serve as permanent containers for books that do not qualify for costly treatment. The self-closing wrapper provides easy access to the item inside. For materials less than an inch thick, an enclosure such as the *two-part folder* (pp. 99–105) would be more suitable.

Materials:
1. Map folder stock .010 for average books, 20 pt. caliper library board for larger, heavy books
2. Adhesive (PVA)
3. Double-sided tape (optional)

Tools:
1. Paper cutter
2. Scissors
3. Bone folder
4. Paste brush
5. Paste container
6. Weights (wrapped bricks)
7. Waste paper
8. Sponge or damp cotton cloth for wiping hands

The self-closing wrapper is made from two separate pieces of map folder stock (one vertical piece and one horizontal piece). For neat folds the grain direction of both pieces must run parallel to the fold.

1. Measure and cut a vertical piece of map folder stock that is equal to the width (W) of the book by two and a half times the height of the book (2½ × H) *plus* twice its thickness (2T). [W × (2½ H + 2T)] (see Figure 153).

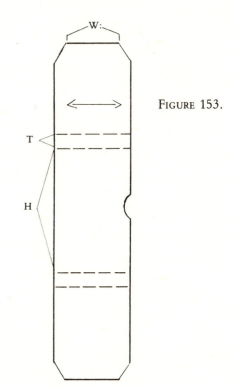

FIGURE 153.

2. Cut a shallow, rounded thumb notch with scissors as illustrated; angle the corners. Place the book in the center of the vertical piece. Fold the extending portions around and crease against the top and bottom edges of the book (see Figure 154).

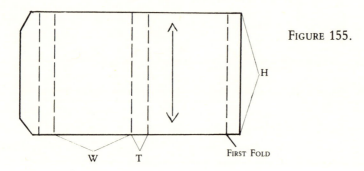

FIGURE 154.

3. Lay the book aside and sharpen the creases with a bone folder.

4. Fold the vertical piece of map folder stock around the book again.

5. Measure and cut a horizontal piece of map folder stock that is the height (H) of the book *wrapped in the vertical piece* by twice the width (2W) *plus* 3 times the thickness (3T) *plus* two inches. [H × (2W + 3T + 2″)] (see Figure 155).

FIGURE 155.

W   T   FIRST FOLD

6. Make the *first fold* a little less than one thickness (T) from the right side edge and stand it straight up.

7. Push the wrapped book against the first fold and proceed to fold and crease the horizontal piece around the book. (see Figure 156).

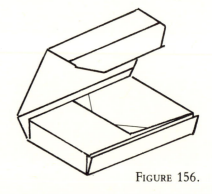

FIGURE 156.

8. Unwrap the book and lay it aside. Sharpen the folds on the horizontal piece of map folder stock and angle the corners of the tuck-in flap.

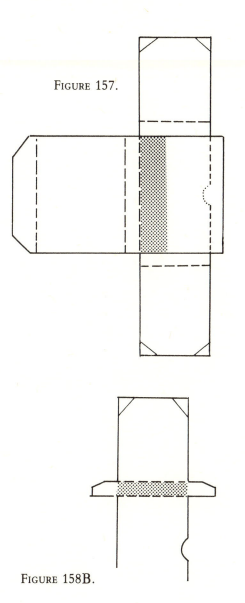

Figure 157.

Figure 158B.

9. Apply adhesive to approximately a third of the middle section of the vertical piece opposite the thumb notch (see Figure 157).

10. Paste the horizontal piece to the vertical piece, as shown (see Figure 157). A strip of double-sided tape can be used instead of adhesive.

11. Wrap the book, folding the flaps in sequence as numbered (see Figure 158A).

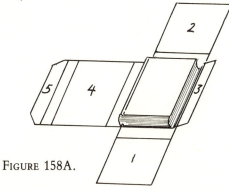

Figure 158A.

Note: To make a wrapper for a very rounded spine, cut a strip of map folder stock to fit between the folds of the vertical piece and let it extend two inches on either side. Affix it in place with adhesive or a strip of double-sided tape (see Figure 158b). Angle the corners, fold the tabs down on the spine and fore-edge of book, then close the flaps.

TWO-PART FOLDER

The two-part folder may be used for thin pamphlets and archival papers (fit into ready-made acid-free envelopes) not more than a quarter of an inch thick.

The envelope should have a top flap to shield against dust and light and should be slit open along one side to permit easy access. If pamphlets or other materials do not fit into the envelope, the two-part folder can be adapted to hold a wrapper.

Boards for the folder may be pre-cut, and the scraps can be cut to the width of the spine and used as spacers, which keep the two cover boards the required distance apart. A three-quarter inch spacer can be used for all two-part folders that hold envelopes.

For two-part folders adapted to contain wrappers, the spacers should be as wide as the thickness of the enclosed item *plus* an extra quarter of an inch, which will allow the folder to fit around the wrapper and close without gaping.

Materials:
1. Acid-free envelopes of various sizes
2. Pressboard
3. Book cloth (Recasing Leather) three or four inches wide
4. Adhesive: 50% PVA and 50% Methyl cellulose
5. Double-sided tape (optional)

Tools:
1. Paper cutter
2. Metal ruler
3. Scissors
4. Bone folder
5. Paste brush
6. Paste container
7. Weights (wrapped bricks)
8. Waste paper
9. Sponge or damp cotton cloth for wiping hands

Two-Part Folder Containing an Envelope

Instructions for a two-part folder that will contain an envelope.
1. Choose an acid-free envelope the appropriate size to fit the item. With the open flap nearest to you, slit the long side to your right with a knife (see Figure 159).

2. Turn the envelope around. Insert the item (see Figure 160). Close the flap.

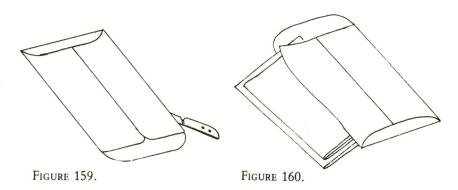

Figure 159.   Figure 160.

Note: Fragile items should be enclosed in a folded piece of acid-free paper to avoid unnecessary handling or rubbing when removing the items or replacing them in the envelope.

3a. Cut two pieces of pressboard the width of the envelope and slightly larger than its height.

  b.Cut a three-quarter inch wide spacer as high as the boards (see Figure 161).

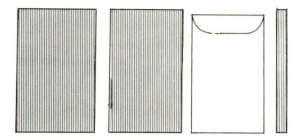

Figure 161.

4. Cut a three inch wide strip of book cloth twice as long as the height of the boards *plus* one-half inch (see Figure 162).

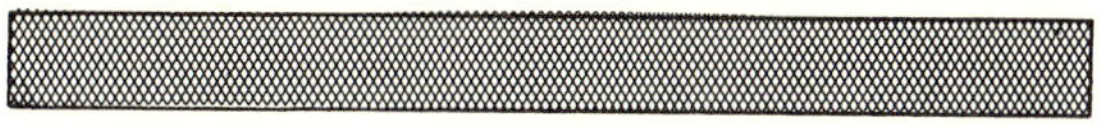

Figure 162.

5. Apply two dabs of adhesive to the spacer (see Figure 163).

Figure 163.

6. Center the spacer on the underside of the cloth strip. About an inch of book cloth should extend beyond three edges of the spacer (see Figure 164). With a little practice this step can be done without exact measurement.

Figure 164.

7. Apply adhesive to the book cloth strip as shown in Figure 165.

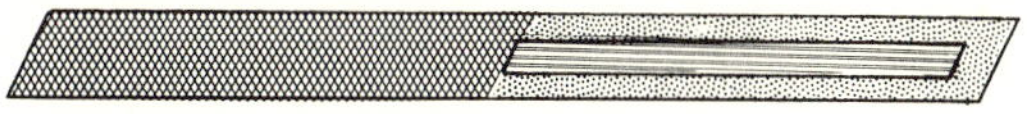

Figure 165.

8. Align one edge of each board up against a side of the spacer, and affix them on the adhesive-coated book cloth (see Figure 166).

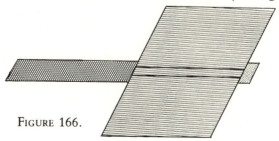

Figure 166.

9. Remove the spacer and turn the one inch wide end of the book cloth in. Rub the cloth (through waste paper) against the board edges with a bone folder. (see Figure 167).

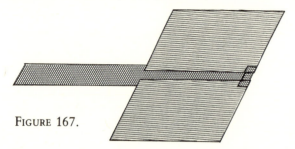

FIGURE 167.

10. Apply adhesive to the extending portion of bookcloth and fold it over to meet the one inch turn-in (see Figure 168).

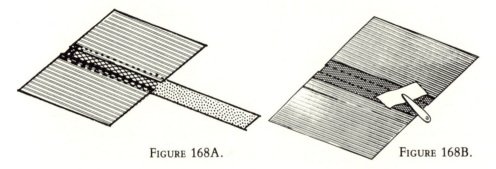

FIGURE 168A.   FIGURE 168B.

11. Remove the item from the envelope.

12. Brush a cross-stroke of adhesive—or use a strip of double-sided tape—on the interior of the bottom board of the folder and paste the *empty* envelope down (see Figure 169).

    Note: The slit side of the envelope must be next to the spine of the folder; otherwise the item may slide out. Let the folder dry completely under a weight before enclosing the item.

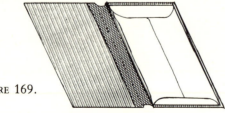

FIGURE 169.

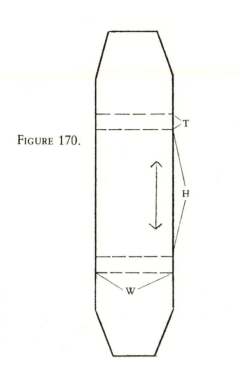

FIGURE 170.

Two-Part Folder Containing a Wrapper

Instructions for a two-part folder that contains a wrapper.

1. Measure and cut a vertical piece of map folder stock the width (W) of the book in one dimension by two and a half times its height *plus* twice its thickness (2½ H + 2T) in the other dimension. Angle the corners. [(W × (2½ H + 2T)] (see Figure 170).

2. Center the book on the piece of map folder stock and fold the extending stock around it, crease the stock against the top and bottom edges of the book (see Figure 171).

FIGURE 171.

3. Lay the book aside and sharpen the creases with a bone folder.

4. Measure and cut a horizontal piece of map folder stock that is the height (H) of the book wrapped in the vertical piece in one dimension by two and a half times its width (2½ W) *plus* twice its thickness (2T) in the other dimension. Angle the corners. [H × (2½W + 2T) (see Figure 172).

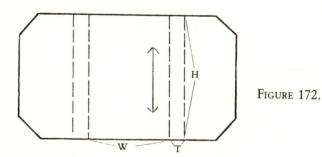

FIGURE 172.

5. With the book wrapped in the vertical piece, center it on the horizontal piece of map folder stock.

6. Fold the extending portions around, creasing them against the spine and fore-edge of the book (see Figure 173).

7. Lay the book aside and sharpen all creases with a bone folder.

8. Brush a cross of adhesive on the middle section of the horizontal piece of map folder stock or use a strip of double-sided tape.

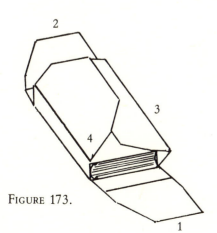

FIGURE 173.

9. Affix the vertical piece to the horizontal piece with adhesive. Weight down with a brick and let dry.

10a. Cut two pieces of pressboard slightly larger than the wrapped item in height and width.

  b. Cut a spacer to the height of the boards equal to the thickness of the wrapped item *plus* one-quarter inch. (see Figure 174).

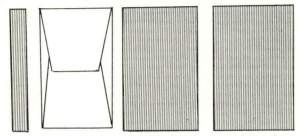

FIGURE 174.

11a. Cut one three-inch strip of book cloth equal to the height of the boards *plus* one inch.

  b. Cut one three-inch strip of book cloth equal to the height of the boards *minus* one-quarter inch.

  Note: To save cloth, the short strip may be cut from a piece of acid-free paper.

12. Apply adhesive to the underside of the *long* cloth strip and center the spacer on the adhesive (see Figure 175).

FIGURE 175.

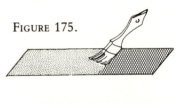

13. Line up the boards, one on each side of the spacer, and paste them down. Rub the boards well, but not the spacer (see Figure 176).

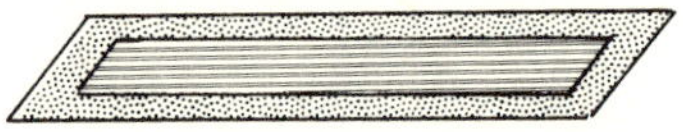

FIGURE 176.

14. Remove the spacer and turn the half inch wide ends of the cloth in. Rub against the inner edges of the boards with a bone folder through waste paper (see Figure 177).

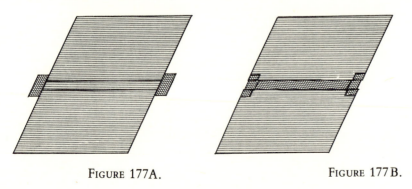

FIGURE 177A.   FIGURE 177B.

15. Apply adhesive to the underside of the *short* cloth strip.

16. Line up the short cloth strip with the turned-in ends of the long cloth strip and paste down. Rub against the inner edges of the boards with a bone folder through waste paper (see Figure 178).

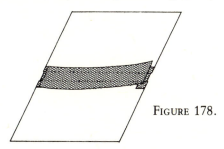

FIGURE 178.

17. Brush a cross of adhesive—or use a strip of double-sided tape—on the interior of the bottom board of the folder and affix the empty wrapper flush with the bottom of the folder. Let the folder adhere completely under a weight before enclosing the item. (See Figure 179).

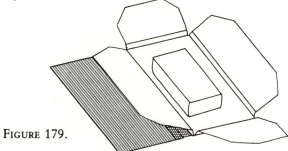

FIGURE 179.

THREE-PART FOLDER

The three-part folder is intended for soft cover or fragile books with damaged corners and edges or worn heads and tails that need a rigid and permanent support. This enclosure is suitable for materials at least *one* inch thick.

When a number of items are to be enclosed, it will speed up production considerably to sort them by size. Anything in the range of 5″ × 7″ to 6″ × 8″, for example, can be put into the same size folder as long as the inner wrapper fits snugly around the object. The inner wrapper should be adhered to the folding case in such a way that the bottom edge is flush with the bottom edge of the case. This will provide added support when the folder stands on the shelf and will help prevent sagging.

Materials:
1. Map folder stock .010
2. Pressboard
3. Book cloth (Recasing Leather) three or four inches wide
4. Adhesive: 50% PVA and 50% Methyl cellulose

Tools:
1. Paper cutter
2. Metal ruler
3. Scissors
4. Bone folder
5. Paste brush
6. Paste container
7. Weights (wrapped bricks)
8. Waste paper
9. Sponge or damp cotton cloth for wiping hands

Make a wrapper following steps 1–9.

1. Measure and cut a vertical piece of map folder stock that is the width (W) of the book in one dimension by two and a half times its height (2½ H) *plus* twice its thickness (2T) in the other dimension. [W × (2½ H + 2T)] (see Figure 180).

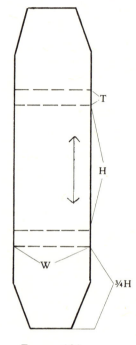

FIGURE 180.

2. Center the book and fold the extending map folder stock around it, crease the stock against the top and bottom edges of the book. (see Figure 181).

FIGURE 181.

3. Lay the book aside and sharpen the creases with a bone folder. Angle the corners.

4. Measure and cut a horizontal piece of map folder stock that is the height (H) of the book wrapped in the vertical piece in one dimension and two and a half times its width (2½ W) *plus* twice its thickness (2T) in the other dimension. [H × (2½ W + 2T)]. (see Figure 182).

5. With the book wrapped in the vertical piece, center it on the horizontal piece of map folder stock.

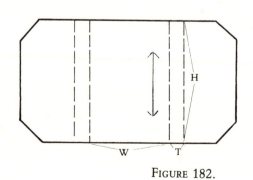

FIGURE 182.

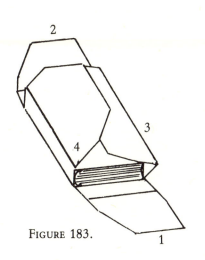

FIGURE 183.

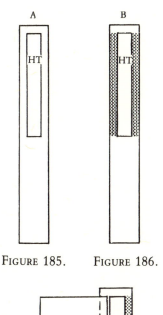

FIGURE 185.   FIGURE 186.

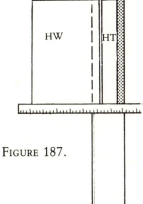

FIGURE 187.

6. Fold the extending portions around, creasing them against the spine and fore-edge of the book. (see Figure 183).

7. Lay the book aside. Sharpen the creases with a bone folder. Angle the corners.

8. Brush a cross of adhesive on the middle section of the horizontal piece of map folder stock or use a strip of double-sided tape.

9. Affix the vertical piece with adhesive on top. Weight down with a brick and let dry.

10. First cut three pieces of pressboard, each slightly larger than the height and width dimensions of the wrapped book. Then cut two pieces of pressboard the same height as the three pieces by the thickness of the wrapped book (see Figure 184).

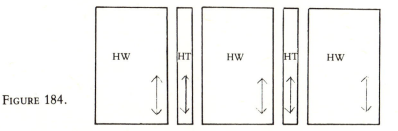

FIGURE 184.

11. Cut two pieces of book cloth that measures twice the height of the HT strips *plus* one inch.

    Note: These two pieces should be three or four inches wide. Use three inch wide strips of book cloth for items up to one and a half inches thick and four inch wide strips for thicker items.

12. Brush adhesive on one side of the HT strips and affix them to the underside of the book cloth, as shown in Figure 185.

    Note: To center the HT strips on the book cloth, mark the middle of pressboard and book cloth strips, then match the marks.

13. Brush mixture on the area indicated in Figure 186.

14. Assemble the case with the help of a steel ruler. Align the ruler against the bottom edge of one HT strip. Set the first HW piece in place, leaving a space of two pressboard *thicknesses* (see Figure 187), two strips of pressboard pasted together can be used as a spacer.

15. Continue to assemble the case by adding an HW piece, an HT strip and the last HW piece. Use the ruler as a guide.

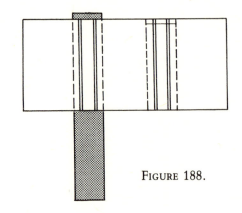

FIGURE 188.

16. Brush adhesive on the extending book cloth and paste into position as illustrated in Figure 188. Rub down well through waste paper with a bone folder.

17. Brush a cross of adhesive (or use double-sided tape) on the middle section of the folding case and affix the wrapper to it flush with the bottom edge of the folder. (see Figure 189).

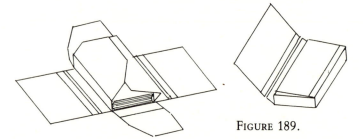

FIGURE 189.

18. Place a weight on top; let the folder dry before enclosing the item.

SLIPCASE I

This type of slipcase is the sturdiest of the enclosures presented in this manual. Because of the expense it should be reserved for large, heavy items more than two inches thick. The inner wrapper, called a *chemise*, protects the spine from light and consequent fading. It also prevents the case from abrading the book while being removed or replaced.

Materials:
1. Map folder stock .010
2. Pressboard
3. Book cloth—Buckram
4. Adhesive: 50% PVA and 50% Methyl cellulose

Tools:
1. Paper cutter
2. Scissors
3. Bone folder
4. Paste brush
5. Paste container
6. Weights (wrapped bricks)
7. Pressing boards
8. Waxed paper
9. Waste paper
10. Sponge or damp cotton cloth for wiping hands.

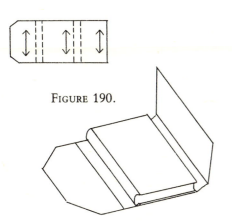

FIGURE 190.

Before making Slipcase I, prepare a chemise:

1. To make a chemise, measure, cut, and fold a horizontal piece of map folder stock that is the height (H) of the book by two and one half times its width, *plus* twice its thickness [H × (2½ W + 2T)]. (see Figure 190).

2. Tightly wrap the book, in its chemise, in waxed paper, for ease of handling and as a guard against adhesive.

3. Measure and cut four pieces of pressboard the height and width of the book. Make sure that the grain runs in the long direction of each piece. Since books are not always square, always take measurements from the largest dimension of the book (see Figure 191).

4. Sandwich the wrapped book between two pieces of pressboard. Set the other two pieces aside (see Figure 192).

FIGURE 191.   FIGURE 192.

5. To measure the thickness for the slipcase, hold the top board down slightly with your hand and crease a paper strip against the lower and upper edges of the two boards at the spine (see Figure 193).

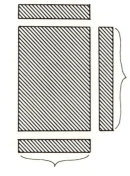

FIGURE 193.

6. Transfer the measurement from the paper onto a piece of pressboard. The pressboard should be slightly longer than the height *plus* twice the width of one of the four pressboards prepared in step 3. Cut the pressboard strip along the T mark (see Figure 194).

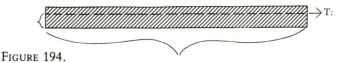

FIGURE 194.

7. Mark off divisions on the pressboard strip for the side pieces using one of the four pressboards (see Figure 195). Cut at the marks.

FIGURE 195.

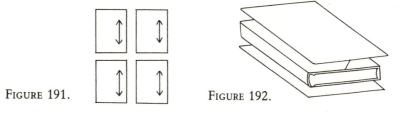

FIGURE 196.

Note: The length of one piece is equal to the height of the piece of pressboard, the length of the other two pieces is equal to the width of the piece of pressboard. (see Figure 196).

8. Cut a book cloth strip to a length equal to the combined length of the three side pieces *plus* two inches. The width equals the thickness *plus* two inches.

9. Divide the book cloth strip in half vertically and horizontally by making tiny creases next to the edges *only*.

10. Draw pencil lines, on the underside of the bookcloth strip, connecting opposite crease marks.

11. Divide and mark the long side strip of pressboard.

12. Coat the long pressboard strip with adhesive and affix it to the underside of the book cloth strip. Match the center marks of both strips (see Figure 197).

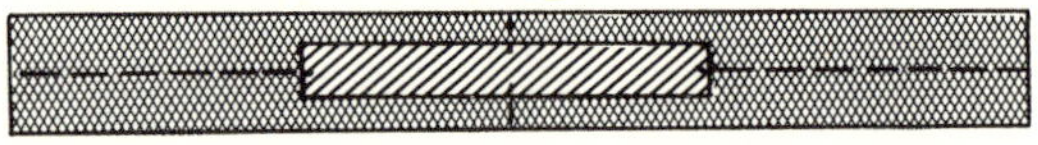

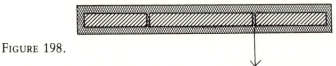

FIGURE 197.

13. Affix the two short side pieces of pressboard to the book cloth strip, with adhesive on either side of the long side strip (see Figure 198). Leave a space between strips equal to the thickness of one piece of pressboard. Place under weights to dry.

FIGURE 198.

14. Fold sections and cut notches at spaces between pressboard pieces, leaving about an eighth of an inch of cloth with which to cover the corners later (see Figure 199).

FIGURE 199.

15. Crease the cloth over the pressboard pieces along the entire length of the strip.

16. Fold the strip around the book block, sandwiched between the two pressboards (see Figure 200).

Note: If the foreedge of the book is not as thick as the spine, slip some scrap pieces of board underneath the pressboard to make it level before pasting the cloth down.

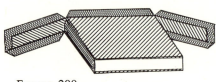

FIGURE 200.

17. Place a weight in the center of the pressboard. Apply adhesive to the underside of the cloth flaps and paste them down (see Figure 201).

18. Brush mixture evenly on one side of the two pressboards set aside earlier and paste it down to the other board being careful to match edges and corners (see Figure 202).

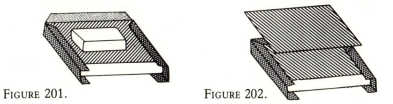

FIGURE 201.   FIGURE 202.

19. Rub well and turn over to repeat steps 17 and 18, then place under a wooden board and bricks to dry.

20. Remove the book (in its chemise). Then cut the extending cloth at the corners.

21. Apply adhesive and turn the cloth in (see Figure 203). Dry thoroughly.

22. Cut thumb notches with a pair of sharp scissors (see Figure 204).

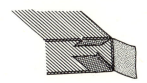
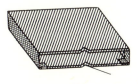

FIGURE 203.   FIGURE 204.

23. Remove the waxed paper from the book unit and slide the book wrapped in the chemise into the slipcase.

SLIPCASE II

Slipcase II, unlike Slipcase I, is lighter, more economical and best suited for smaller books. The best material for making slipcase II is *map folder stock*, which renders a pliable, close-fitting enclosure. The sides of the enclosure expand outward to allow easy grasping and removal of the enclosed book, without abrasion.

Materials:
1. Map folder stock (Library board can be substituted), 10 or 20 point caliper
2. Double-sided tape

Tools:
1. Steel ruler
2. Bone folder
3. Paper cutter
4. Scissors

Instructions for preparing Slipcase II:
1. Cut a piece of map folder stock to approximately two inches *larger* than twice the width of the book by three times its height *plus* twice its thickness. The grain should run parallel to the *shorter edges*. This is the *horizontal* piece [(2W + 2″) × (3H + 2T)]. Divide it in half and mark at each short edge (see Figure 205).

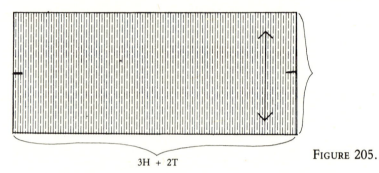

3H + 2T

FIGURE 205.

2. Align a steel ruler on the dividing marks and score along this line with a bone folder (see Figure 206).

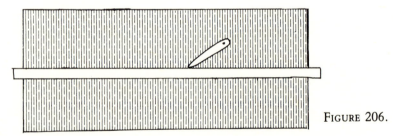

FIGURE 206.

3. Fold along the score and sharpen with a bone folder (see Figure 207).

FIGURE 207.

4. Measure and cut the folded piece to the width of the book. Center the book on the folded piece (see Figure 208).

FIGURE 208.

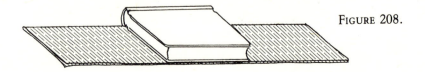

5. Crease the extending portions against the top and bottom edges of the book (see Figure 209).

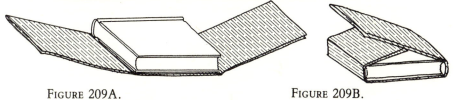

FIGURE 209A.   FIGURE 209B.

6. Lay the book aside. Sharpen the creases with a bone folder. Trim one-quarter inch from the edges of flap A and angle the lower open edges (see Figure 210).

FIGURE 210.

7. Cut a piece of map folder stock to four times the width *plus* two book thicknesses by the height of the book [(4W + 2T) × H]. The grain should run parallel to the *shorter* edges. This is the *vertical* piece. Fold this piece in half (see Figure 211).

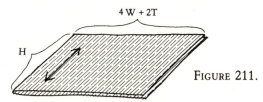

4 W + 2T

H

FIGURE 211.

8. Align the spine of the book with the folded edge of the vertical piece of map folder stock (see Figure 212).

9. Crease the extending part around the fore-edge of the book (see Figure 213).

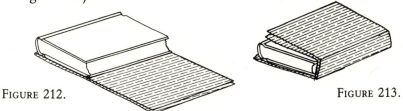

FIGURE 212.   FIGURE 213.

10. Lay the book aside and sharpen the creases with a bone folder. Mark the outer vertical flap with a pencilled D and the inner one with a C (see Figure 214).

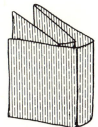

FIGURE 214.

11. Trim flap D to three-quarters of the width of the book and angle the corners. Apply a thin strip of double-sided tape to flap C (see Figure 215). *Do not remove the wrapper paper strip from the tape yet.*

Note: You have now prepared both a vertical and a horizontal piece of map folder stock (see Figure 216).

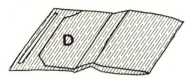

FIGURE 215.

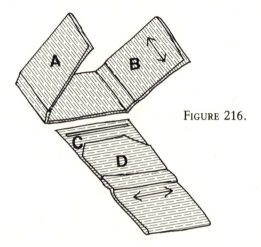

FIGURE 216.

12. Unfold both pieces of stock. Turn the vertical piece over and place flap C on the lower middle section of the horizontal piece (see Figure 217). Make sure that the fold of flap C is aligned with the lower edge of the horizontal piece. Hold in position while peeling the wrapper paper from the double-sided tape. Press down firmly on flap C over the taped area.

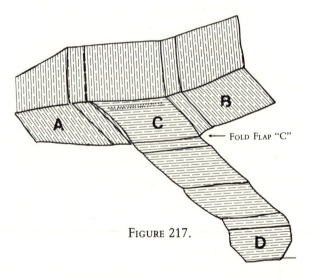

FIGURE 217.

13. Fold over the upper portion of the horizontal piece (see Figure 218).

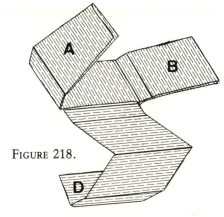

FIGURE 218.

14. Bring the vertical piece up and over (see Figure 219).

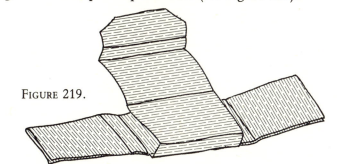

FIGURE 219.

15. Tuck flap A into flap B (see Figure 220).

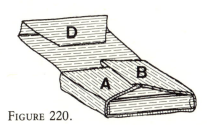

FIGURE 220.

16. Measure and cut a strip of map folder stock slightly narrower than the spine of the slipcase. The length should equal the height of the slipcase *plus* three inches. Place the strip along the spine and crease it against the head and tail edges of the slipcase (see Figure 221). Crease and tuck the two short ends of the strip between the doubled map folder stock at the head and tail.

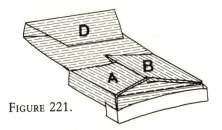

FIGURE 221.

17. Fold the extending portion of the vertical piece over flaps A and B and around the spine. Tuck in flap D (see Figure 222).

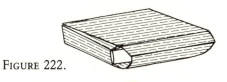

FIGURE 222.

SLIPCASE III (FOR BOOKS WITH DETACHED BOARDS)

In most libraries, books with detached boards are tied with cotton tape or held together with rubber bands. Cotton tape, even tightly tied, can loosen, permitting the boards to shift causing damage to the bookblock. The use of rubber bands, which rot and become sticky as they deteriorate, can cut into the bookblock, and should be avoided at all costs.

For books that will not be immediately rebound, and in particular those that may eventually be rebound or restored *using original parts*, slipcase III (for books with detached boards) is an excellent method of preservation. Easy access to the enclosed book is permitted by loosening two flaps which also prevent the boards from being separated from the book and subsequently becoming lost.

Because it is easy and inexpensive to produce and does *not* require liquid adhesive, this type of slipcase can be used for materials at many levels of importance.

Materials:
1. Map folder stock or Bristol board
2. Acid-free wrapping paper
3. Double-sided tape

Tools:
1. Ruler
2. Bone folder
3. Paper cutter
4. Scissors

Instructions for preparing Slipcase III:
1. Measure and cut a piece of wrapping paper to twice the height of the book by four times its width *plus* one thickness. [2H × (4W + T)] (see Figure 223).

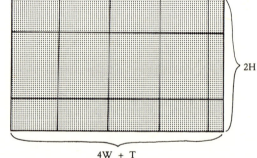

FIGURE 223.

2. Center one of the detached boards on the wrapping paper, along the short edge, so that equal portions extend at top and bottom. Crease the extending portions of the paper over the board and fold along the long sides of the wrapping paper (see Figure 224).

FIGURE 224.

3. Measure the thickness (spine width) of the book and transfer this measurement to each short edge (see Figure 225).

FIGURE 225.

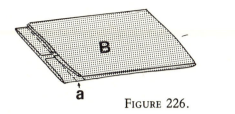

FIGURE 226.

4. Bring side edge of B over to line a. Align the top and bottom edges. Fold and crease (see Figure 226).

5. Next bring the edge side A over to line b. Align the top and bottom. Fold and crease (see Figure 227). This establishes the spine area (see Figure 228).

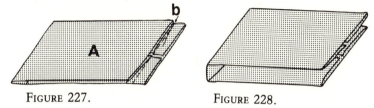

FIGURE 227.   FIGURE 228.

6. Fold each short edge over to approximately one-eighth inch away from *its* spine crease. Make sure that the top and bottom edges are aligned. Fold and crease (see Figure 229). This completes the formation of pockets one and two.

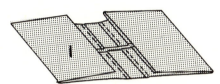

FIGURE 229.

7. Insert the detached boards in pockets 1 and 2. (see Figure 230).

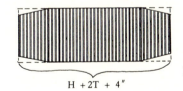

FIGURE 230.

8. Cut a strip of map folder stock wide enough to fit between the spine fold and the fore-edge fold of pocket 2 (see Figure 231). The length of the strip equals the height of the book *plus* twice its thickness *plus* four inches (H + 2T + 4"). Angle the corners.

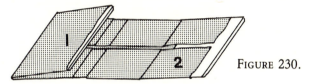

H + 2T + 4"

FIGURE 231.

9. Affix the map folder stock strip under packet 2 using double-sided tape. Make sure that equal portions extend at top and bottom (see Figure 232).

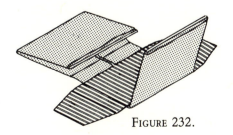

FIGURE 232.

10. Fold pocket 2 down and place the book block on top (see Figure 233). Then fold pocket 1 over the book block.

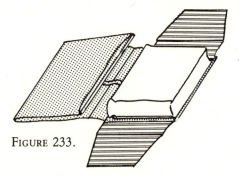

FIGURE 233.

Note: Both boards, in their respective pockets should fit snugly against the shoulder of the book block.

11. Fold the extending map folder stock flaps up and around the book. Crease the folds. Tuck the flaps in as shown (see Figure 234).

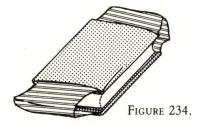

FIGURE 234.

Pamphlet bindings are used for soft-covered materials that need support, but are not generally recommended for items that are oversize, more than three-quarters of an inch thick, rare, or fragile. *Two-part and three-part folders* are suggested for larger, rare, and fragile items.

It is preferable to preserve pamphlets in-house, using the methods covered here, which can be adjusted to fit the wide variety of binding styles found on soft-covered materials. However, as a preservation staff and a good paper cutter are essential for handling large quantities of materials, many libraries prefer to use ready-made pamphlet binders which are available from library suppliers. These binders are adequate if one additional step is taken: Sewing the pamphlets into a folded cloth strip before inserting them into the binders. Working assembly-line fashion on groups of pamphlets of the same size can make this method more efficient. Repeating one step several times before going on to the next not only helps improve skills, but also allows time for adhesives to dry, without slowing down the work flow.

Sort the pamphlets according to dimensions and binding style. Boards and cloth should be cut in quantity to the same dimensions for pamphlets that vary only slightly in height and width.

Set aside pamphlets which have torn or detached covers but are worth saving. Treatment for these pamphlets is described in this chapter, pp. 132–134. "Reattaching Pamphlet Covers."

Note: The adhesive referred to throughout this chapter is equal parts of PVA and methyl cellulose.

The value and importance of the items to be bound, as well as the availability of materials, should be taken into consideration before deciding on the type of book cloth to use. In terms of price and quality, book cloth bought by the full yard is generally a better buy, if it must be cut into strips it may prove less economical. When cutting strips from large pieces of cloth, the long edge of the strip should run in the same direction as the selvage edge, which is also the direction of the grain.

Pyroxylin-coated Recasing Leather used for pamphlet binding, available in 25 yard rolls precut to a three inch width, offers certain advantages. It can be:

—used with a minimum of waste
—handled with ease
—wiped clean with a damp cotton rag
—stored easily

Additional advantages of pyroxylin-coated book cloth are resistance to mold and wear from shelving and handling. Starch-filled bookcloth and buckram can be substituted. Starch-filled bookcloth is more aesthetically pleasing and adheres to materials rapidly easily.

Materials:
1. Pressboard
2. Recasing Leather in 25-yard roll, three inches wide, or book cloth such as starch-filled linen or buckram by the yard
3. Linen thread, size 18/3
4. Adhesive PVA and methyl cellulose
5. Waste paper
6. Waxed paper
7. Japanese paper (Okawara)

Tools:
1. Paper cutter
2. Mat knife and heavy metal straight edge
3. Scissors
4. Bone folder
5. Paste brush (polyester, one-inch wide, flat)
6. Paste bowl
7. Weights (wrapped bricks)
8. Needle
9. Awl and mallet or hand drill with one-sixteenth-inch bit
10. Paper clips
11. Pencil
12. Scrap paper or several layers of cardboard to protect working table surface
13. Damp cotton cloth to wipe hands

SINGLE SIGNATURE PAMPHLET BINDING

A single signature pamphlet has several folded leaves inserted, one into another, to form one signature; and it is sewn or stapled, through the fold, to a limp cover. Leave the original sewing as is, but remove all staples before proceeding. Staples are best removed with a blunt knife.

1. Cut two pieces of press board to the height of the pamphlet *plus* a quarter inch by the width of the pamphlet *minus* a quarter inch

2. Open the pamphlet to the center fold of the signature and insert a strip of waste paper. Later this will aid in quickly locating the center (see Figure 235).

FIGURE 235.

3. Cut a two and a half inch wide strip of book cloth or use a three-inch precut strip of recasing leather. The length of the strip should equal twice the height of the board *plus* one inch.

Note: Measure the strip by positioning one of the precut boards on the wrong side of the book cloth strip, flush with one long edge of the cloth and an inch away from one short edge. Draw lines on the book cloth against the short edges of the board (see Figure 236). Move the board along to line up with the second pencil line and draw a third. Cut the cloth strip at this line.

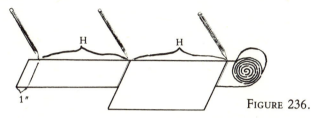

Figure 236.

4. With the cloth strip in front of you, right side up, fold it in half lengthwise. The wrong side, *bearing the pencil lines*, should be facing you.

5. Place the book cloth strip around the spine of the pamphlet, centering the pamphlet between the two pencil lines. A little more than an inch will extend at the tail of the pamphlet and the long end will extend at the head of the pamphlet (see Figure 237).

6. Hold the cloth strip in position and open the pamphlet to the center fold as marked by the piece of paper. Fasten the cloth—with paper clips—to prevent it from shifting position (see Figure 238). Remove the marker.

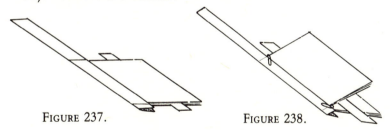

Figure 237.   Figure 238.

7. Inspect the original sewing or the staple holes to determine whether they can be reused.

Note: For pamphlets up to ten inches high, three sewing holes will suffice. For larger pamphlets use five holes. Choose evenly spaced holes— one should be in the middle, the other two approximately an inch away from the head and tail. When five sewing holes are used, the two additional holes should be situated between the center and the head and tail holes. The five-hole sewing method is explained in the Multiple Signature Pamphlet Binding section pp. 125–126. If it is necessary to make new holes, see Chapter 4, Working Tips, pp. 36–37, instructions for piercing evenly spaced holes using a jig for an easy method of spacing holes.

8. To make sewing easy, first pierce the pamphlet pages and the book cloth strip with a needle. Make sure the holes are in the exact center of the fold (see Figure 239).

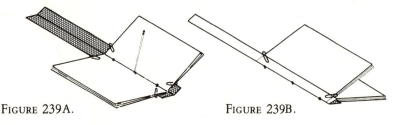

FIGURE 239A.   FIGURE 239B.

9. To sew, thread a needle with linen thread slightly longer than twice the height of the pamphlet. Sew from the inside of the pamphlet out through the center hole (1) leaving the tail about three inches long (see Figure 240).

10. Sew through hole 2. The needle is now on the inside (see Figure 241).

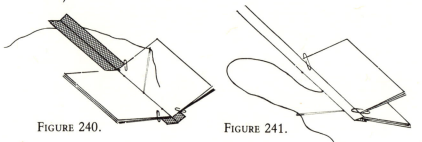

FIGURE 240.   FIGURE 241.

11. Skip the middle hole (1) and sew through hole 3, bringing the needle to the outside (see Figure 242).

12. Push the needle through the center hole back to the inside. Remove needle and paper clips. (see Figure 243).

Note: The long stitch between hole 2 and hole 3 runs between the two loose ends.

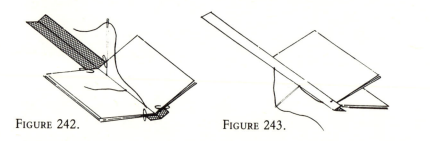

FIGURE 242.   FIGURE 243.

13. Gently pull the thread ends to tighten the sewing. Make a square knot (see Chapter 4, Knots, p. 37) and trim ends, leaving half inch tails (see Figure 244). Close the pamphlet.

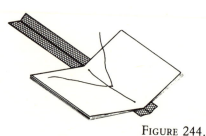

FIGURE 244.

14. To attach the boards, slip strips of waste paper and waxed paper between the cloth and the pamphlet. The waste paper must be next to the cloth and the waxed paper next to the pamphlet. (see Figure 245).

15. Keeping at least half an inch away from the spine, brush an even amount of adhesive onto the cloth. Don't worry if the adhesive goes a little beyond the designated area. *Remove the waste paper immediately.* Leave the waxed paper in place (see Figure 246).

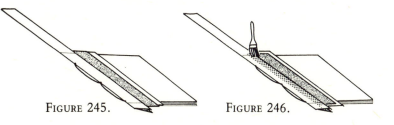

FIGURE 245.   FIGURE 246.

16. Brush adhesive onto an area about an inch wide on the long side of the precut board, to assure a good bond.

17. Position the board between the pencil lines on the cloth strip, adhesive to adhesive, so that it extends an eighth of an inch at the fore-edge. Align the board by inserting a strip of paper at the fore-edge of the pamphlet, letting it protrude an eighth of an inch, and lining board up with this strip (see Figure 247). You can also measure by eye.

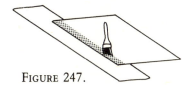

FIGURE 247.

18. Press the board down firmly and rub the adhesive-coated area through the waste paper with a bone folder. Wipe off any excess adhesive that seeps out.

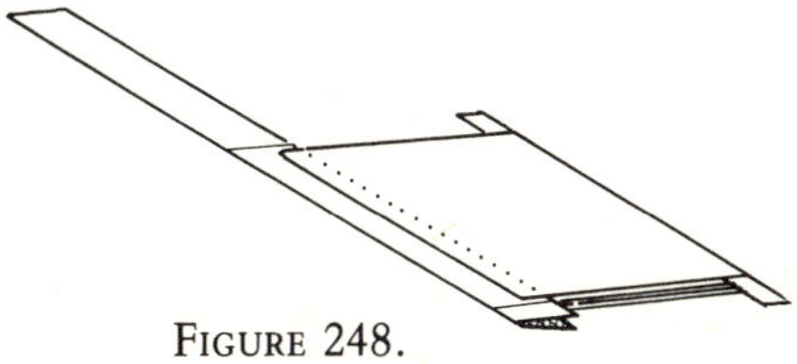

19. Turn the pamphlet over and repeat steps 14–18 (see Figures 245–248).

FIGURE 248.

20. Place a weight on top and let dry for 20 minutes (see Figure 249).

21. Remove the weight. Open the pamphlet to the center and lay it flat, face down. Apply mixture to the extending pieces of cloth (see Figure 250).

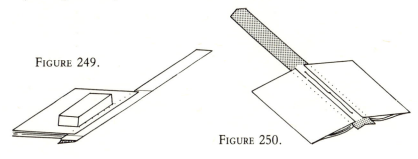

FIGURE 249.

FIGURE 250.

22. Turn the short section over first and rub down well (see Figure 251A).

23. Turn the long section over, lining up the edges with the short turn-in (see Figure 251B).

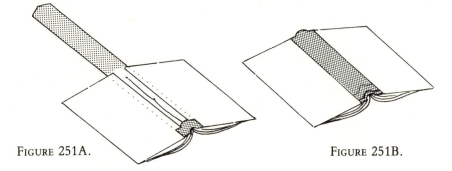

FIGURE 251A.   FIGURE 251B.

24. Close the pamphlet and, using a bone folder, rub down well through waste paper. Wipe off any excess adhesive (see Figure 252).

25. Place a weight on top of the pamphlet and let dry for at least 20 minutes (see Figure 253).

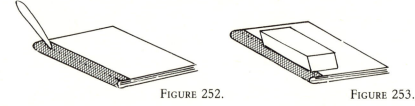

FIGURE 252.   FIGURE 253.

26. To establish a crease, open one cover and bend it back toward the spine. Where the board ends, flatten the bend with a bone folder (see Figure 254). Repeat on the other side. This will make the covers open easily.

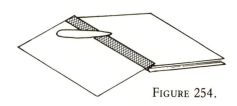

FIGURE 254.

MULTIPLE SIGNATURE PAMPHLET BINDING

A pamphlet made up of multiple signatures, linked together by sewing, opens well. If possible this feature should be preserved. With the original sewing still intact, re-sewing through the first, middle, and last signature is sufficient to attach the pamphlet to a cloth hinge. Pamphlets with as many as five signatures are sewn to the cloth hinge through the first and last signatures only. Should the original sewing of the pamphlet be weak or broken, the pamphlet can be completely resewn. This is generally considered very time-consuming, but there are instances when resewing is necessary to save the inner margins. A method of resewing pamphlets or small books, without using a sewing frame, is described on pp. 139–142. For multiple signature pamphlets with defective sewing and wide margins, see *Side Sewing with New Holes* in this chapter. pp. 127–128.

The materials and tools are the same as those listed at the beginning of this chapter, p. 120.

1. Cut a two and one-half inch wide strip of buckram or other book cloth or use three inch wide precut Recasing Leather from a roll. The strip should equal the height of the pamphlet.

2. Center the pamphlet and crease the book cloth around the edges of the spine. The wrong side of the cloth should face you (see Figure 255).

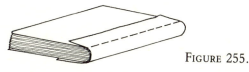

FIGURE 255.

3. Hold the cloth strip in position and open the pamphlet to the middle of the first signature. Fasten the cloth strip to the pamphlet with two paper clips (see Figure 256). This will prevent the cloth strip from moving out of position. Repeat this step at the middle and last signatures.

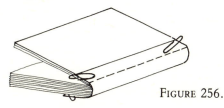

FIGURE 256.

4. Open the pamphlet to the first signature. Pierce five evenly spaced holes with an awl (see Figure 257). (See Chapter 4, pp. 36, 37.) Repeat this process with the other signatures.

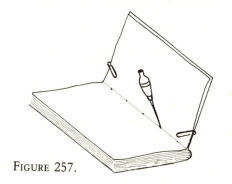

FIGURE 257.

5. Thread a needle with a linen thread six times as long as the pamphlet is high.

6. From the outside of the pamphlet, sew in through the center of the signature (see Figure 258). Leave a tail about three inches long.

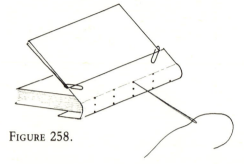

FIGURE 258.

7. Sew, following the direction of the arrow (see Figure 259).

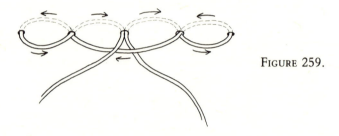

FIGURE 259.

8. Gently pull the two loose ends after each signature is sewn to tighten the sewing; make a square knot (see Figure 260).

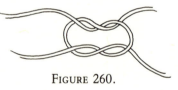

FIGURE 260.

9. Continue the sewing by pushing the needle through the center of the middle signature (see Figure 261). Proceed as described in step 7.

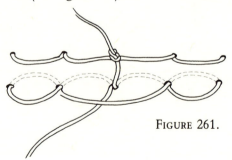

FIGURE 261.

10. Secure the sewing by tying the two loose ends into a square knot (see Figure 262).

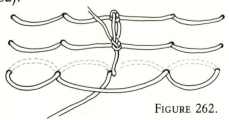

FIGURE 262.

11. Sew through the center of the *last* signature.

12. Secure sewing with a square knot and trim ends evenly, leaving half inch tails.

13. To make the case for the pamphlet, turn to pp. 130–132, "Making the Case for Pamphlets Consisting of Single Leaves or Multiple Signatures."

PAMPHLETS CONSISTING OF A GROUP OF SINGLE LEAVES

A pamphlet consisting of a group of single leaves, rather than signatures, usually is originally adhesive-bound or stapled. Any staples should be removed, but the adhesive may be left. The pamphlet can be *side-sewn* if the inner margin is at least five-eighths of an inch wide. Pamphlets frequently turn up which, in an earlier attempt to preserve and strengthen them, were laced to highly acidic covers, using shoestrings run through enormous holes along the side of the pamphlet. These pamphlets should be removed from their covers. Test the paper by bending a corner back and forth several times, to determine if it is strong enough to be re-sewn. If it breaks, it is better to put the pamphlet into a two-part folder (see page 100).

SIDE SEWING WITH NEW HOLES

1. Cut a strip of buckram or other book cloth two and a half inches wide by the height of the pamphlet.

2. Crease the book cloth around the spine of the pamphlet with the wrong side of the book cloth facing you (see Figure 263A).

3. Fasten the book cloth to the front and back cover of the pamphlet with paper clips. Place a weight on the pamphlet (see Figure 263B).

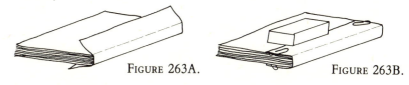

FIGURE 263A.   FIGURE 263B.

4. Mark the sewing holes on the book cloth with a pencil, one-quarter inch away from the edge of the spine (see Figure 264).

Note: The new sewing holes should be clear of the original sewing holes. The original holes can usually be felt through the book cloth and avoided.

FIGURE 264.

5. Make holes at the pencil marks with a mallet and awl (see Figure 265) or use a hand drill with a one-sixteenth inch drill bit. Remove the weight.

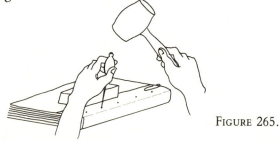

FIGURE 265.

6. Thread a needle with linen thread three times as long as the height of the pamphlet. Start by sewing through the middle hole (see Figure 266). Leave a tail about three inches long.

FIGURE 266.

7. Sew, following the direction of the arrows (see Figure 267).

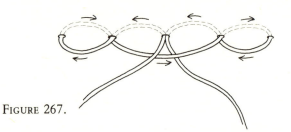

FIGURE 267.

8. Remove the paper clips and gently pull the two loose ends to tighten the sewing. Make a square knot.

9. To make the case for the pamphlet, turn to pp. 130–132, "Making the Case for Pamphlets Consisting of Single Leaves or Multiple Signatures.

SIDE SEWING WITH EXISTING HOLES

1. Cut a two and a half inch wide strip of buckram or other book cloth to the height of the pamphlet. Center and crease the book cloth around the spine of the pamphlet with the wrong side of the book cloth facing you (see Figure 268).

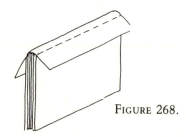

FIGURE 268.

2. Fasten the book cloth to the front of the pamphlet with paper clips (see Figure 269).

3. Turn the pamphlet over to the back and hold it in place with a weight. Lift and bend the book cloth toward the spine so you can see and feel the previous sewing or stapling holes. Push a needle or awl through the holes to mark their position on the book cloth fastened with paper clips to the front of the pamphlet (see Figure 270).

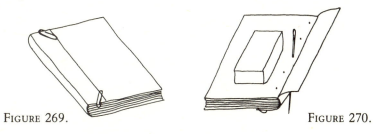

FIGURE 269.   FIGURE 270.

4. Remove the weight and fasten the book cloth to the back of the pamphlet with paper clips (see Figure 271).

5. Turn the pamphlet over. Once more, push a needle or awl through the holes to mark their position on the book cloth fastened with paper clips to the back of the pamphlet (see Figure 272).

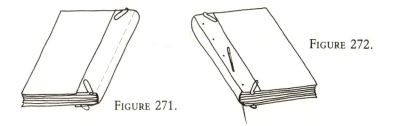

FIGURE 272.

FIGURE 271.

6. Thread a needle with linen thread three times as long as the height of the pamphlet. Start by sewing through the middle hole. Leave a tail about three inches long (see Figure 273).

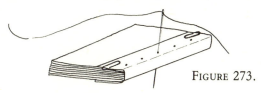

FIGURE 273.

7. Sew, following the directions of the arrow (see Figure 274).

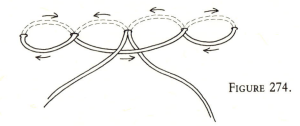

FIGURE 274.

8. Remove the paper clips and gently pull the two loose ends to tighten the sewing. Make a square knot.

9. To make the case for the pamphlet, turn to pp. 130–132, "Making the Case for Pamphlets Consisting of Single Leaves or Multiple Signatures."

MAKING THE CASE FOR PAMPHLETS CONSISTING OF SINGLE LEAVES OR MULTIPLE SIGNATURES

1. To make the case for the pamphlet, cut two pieces of board to the height of the pamphlet *plus* one quarter inch by the width of the pamphlet *minus* one-quarter inch (see Figure 275).

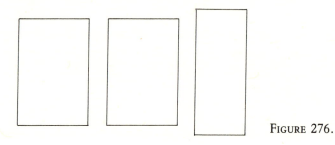

FIGURE 275.

2. Cut a strip of book cloth to the height of the boards *plus* one inch (see Figure 276) by two and one-half inches wide.

FIGURE 276.

3. Make sharp lengthwise creases at the top and bottom of the book cloth strip to mark the middle (see Figure 277).

FIGURE 277.

4. Cut a pressboard strip to the height of the covers by as wide as the pamphlet is thick *plus* one inch. Mark its middle at top and bottom (see Figure 278).

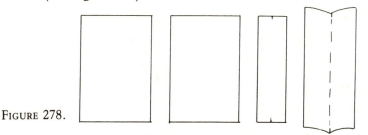

FIGURE 278.

Note: The strip is used as a spacer while attaching the board covers to the cloth strip. After this is done, the spacer is lifted and put aside. When many pamphlets are being bound, there's no need to cut a new spacer for each pamphlet. Instead the same spacers can be used over and over again. They may be shorter or longer than the board covers. A width of one and one-quarter inch for thin pamphlets and one and one-half inches for thicker *ones will do.*

5. Apply two dabs of adhesive to the spacer, and center it on the wrong side of the book cloth strip by matching creases and middle marks. Equal portions of book cloth should extend at head and tail (see Figure 279).

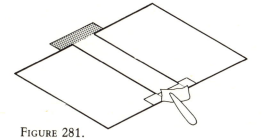

FIGURE 279.

6. Apply adhesive to the entire length of the book cloth strip on one side of the spacer. Place one side of the cover board against one side of the spacer, so that the spacer and cover are aligned at the bottom. As soon as the board is in the right position, weight it down with a brick (see Figure 280).

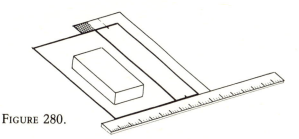

FIGURE 280.

7. Repeat step 6 on the other side of the spacer. Then remove the spacer.

8. After the boards have dried for at least 20 minutes, remove the bricks. Apply a little more adhesive to the extending cloth at head and tail, turn it in, and affix it to the board. Rub with a bone folder through waste paper and let dry (see Figure 281).

FIGURE 281.

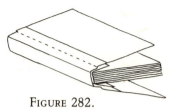

Figure 282.

9. Position the pamphlet inside the case, so that the book cloth strip which was sewn around the pamphlet, matches the turn-ins of the book cloth strip affixed around the boards (see Figure 282).

10. Open the cover and place a weight on the pamphlet. Slip strips of waxed paper and waste paper underneath the book cloth hinge. The waxed paper should be next to the pamphlet and the waste paper next to the book cloth. Apply adhesive to the cloth hinge (see Figure 283).

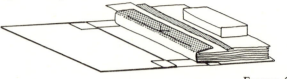

Figure 283.

11. *Remove and discard the waste paper.* Put the weights aside. Hold the pamphlet down firmly with your hand and close the front cover over the adhesive-coated book cloth (see Figure 284).

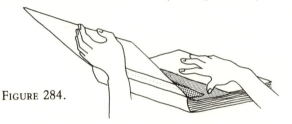

Figure 284.

12. Rub down well and draw the bone folder back and forth along the edge of the board, which you can feel underneath the book cloth. Let dry under a weight, then repeat on the other side.

13. After at least fifteen minutes open one cover and bend it back toward the spine. Where the board ends, flatten the bend with a bone folder to establish a crease (see Figure 285). Repeat on the other side. This will make the covers open easily.

Figure 285.

RE-ATTACHING PAMPHLET COVERS

Worn and detached original pamphlet covers, which are worth saving, can be strengthened and re-attached. Following the instructions for backing or laminating on pp. 66–70, back *or* laminate the covers if they are torn and weak. After the covers are dry, proceed as follows.

1. Trim the covers all around, except on the spine edge. Let enough Japanese paper extend there to fold around and cover the spine (see Figure 286).

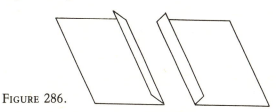

FIGURE 286.

FIGURE 287.

2. Cut a strip of Okawara paper (Japanese paper) to the height of the covers by as wide as the pamphlet is thick, *plus* one inch (see Figure 287). Make a sharp little crease lengthwise at the top and bottom of the strip to indicate the middle.

Note: These strips may be precut to one or one and a quarter inch widths for the thin pamphlets, one and a half inch widths for the thicker pamphlets. They can then be trimmed to the length needed.

3. Remove any loose bits of glue and paper from the spine, then apply adhesive (see Figure 288).

4. Paste the Okawara paper strip to the spine, centering the creases. Smooth the strip down until it adheres (see Figure 289). You now have a front and back hinge extending from the spine.

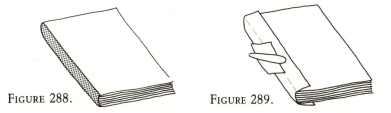

FIGURE 288.   FIGURE 289.

5. Insert strips of waxed paper and waste paper underneath the Okawara paper hinge. The waxed paper should be next to the pamphlet and the waste paper next to the hinge (see Figure 290).

6. Apply adhesive to the front Okawara paper hinge and to the spine. *Remove and discard the waste paper strip (see Figure 291).*

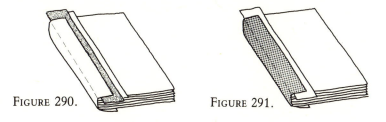

FIGURE 290.   FIGURE 291.

7. Position the front cover and affix it onto the Okawara paper hinge (see Figure 292). Paste the extending Japanese paper hinge over the spine and smooth it down.

8. Turn the pamphlet over and repeat steps 5, 6, and 7.

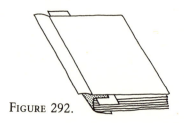

FIGURE 292.

USING READY-MADE PAMPHLET BINDERS

Ready-made pamphlet binders provide a free-swinging adhesive-binding strip which is stitched lengthwise through the middle to the pamphlet binder (see Figure 293).

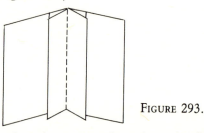

FIGURE 293.

The strip is moistened with water and stuck to the front and back covers of the pamphlet. Besides the fact that this strip often does not adhere properly, all the stress of opening and closing is concentrated on the covers. Many pamphlets do not have covers substantial enough to withstand the strain. The covers may break along the binding strip edge, and often the book block separates itself and has to be dealt with again. This is not efficient in the long run. The following procedure offers a solution to the problem. It does require some additional steps, but the results are well worth the effort.

1. Sew pamphlets to two and a half inch buckram or other book cloth strips, cut to the height of the pamphlets, or use three inch pre-cut book cloth from a roll. Follow the sewing instructions given earlier in this chapter, pp. 120–130. Use the instructions for single signatures, multiple signature *or* side sewing whichever is required (see Figures 294A, B, C).

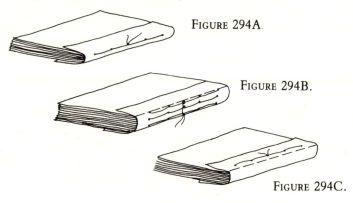

FIGURE 294A.

FIGURE 294B.

FIGURE 294C.

2. Select a ready-made pamphlet binder of appropriate size, no more than half an inch larger than the pamphlet at top, bottom, and fore-edge. Position the pamphlet inside the binder. The overlaps or squares should be even on three sides. (If the pamphlet is heavy, line it up flush with the bottom edge of the binder to avoid sagging.) Open the front cover of the binder and hold the pamphlet in place with a weight.

3. Slip a piece of waste paper between the binder and the binding strip and a piece of waxed paper between the pamphlet and the cloth (see Figure 295).

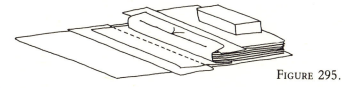

FIGURE 295.

4. Apply adhesive to the binding strip. *Remove and discard the waste paper*, but leave the waxed paper in place (see Figure 296).

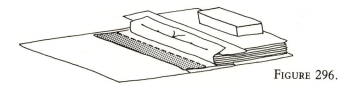

FIGURE 296.

5. Hold the pamphlet down firmly with your hand, and close the front cover so that the adhesive-covered side of the binding strip will adhere to the book cloth strip sewn around the pamphlet (see Figure 297). Rub down and let dry under a weight for 20 minutes. Repeat on the other side.

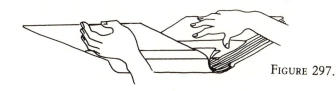

FIGURE 297.

The bristol binding has been designed for use with sewn pamphlets and books of fewer than ten signatures made of paper that is not brittle. This type of binding is a solution for pamphlets or books with narrow gutter margins and can be successfully executed with simple tools.

Materials:
1. Acid-free paper
2. Acid-free bristol board
3. Pressboard (optional)
4. Book cloth
5. Unbleached Irish linen thread (size 30)
6. Japanese paper (Okawara)
7. Adhesive: 50% PVA and 50% Methyl cellulose
8. Waxed paper
9. Unprinted newsprint

Tools:
1. Paper cutter or mat knife
2. Scissors
3. Bone folder
4. Paste brush
5. Paste bowl
6. Weights (wrapped bricks)
7. Needle
8. Awl
9. Pencil
10. Steel ruler
11. Pressing boards
12. Paper clips

If the sewing is no longer intact, it is not difficult to resew the signature without a sewing frame. Take the pamphlet or book apart, signature by signature, without tearing them. Remove all the old sewing thread and, using your thumb and forefinger, carefully rub off any loose adhesive from the spine folds. Check the outer folds of the signatures. If they are weak or torn, guard them as described in Chapter 6, p. 65.

1. Fold two pieces of acid-free paper in half and cut them to the dimensions of the signatures (see Figure 298). They will become the front and back flyleaves and, during the preparation for sewing, should be counted as signatures.

FIGURE 298.

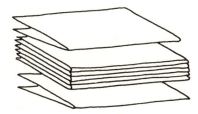

2. Cut two strips of book cloth to the height of the signatures by an inch wide.

3. Apply adhesive to a one-eighth inch wide area along the folded or spine edge of the flyleaves, (see Figure 299) then affix the book cloth strip to each of the flyleaves with the underside of the book cloth facing up.

FIGURE 299.

4. Using a bone folder, rub down well through a piece of waste paper (see Figure 300).

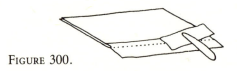

FIGURE 300.

5. Place between clean sheets of waste paper and place under a pressing board and weight. Allow the adhesive to dry.

6. Fold the book cloth around the flyleaves and add them to the stack of signatures, making sure that the signatures are in the right order (see Figures 301A and 301B).

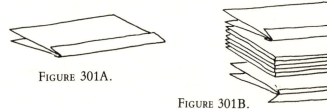

FIGURE 301A.

FIGURE 301B.

Note: Some of the original sewing holes may be reused, but more often it is easier to pierce new holes. To insure evenly spaced holes, cut a strip of bristol to the height of the signatures by about six inches wide. Fold it in half lengthwise and mark the positions for five sewing holes. (See illustrations Chapter 4, p. 36.) Cut a notch in one short edge of the jig (see Figure 302). Always insert the jig in each signature with the notch at the same end.

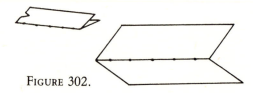

FIGURE 302.

7. Before starting to sew, collate the signatures making sure they are in the right order.

   Note: Signatures are easily turned upside down as they are removed from the stack. Avoid getting the stack out of order by going through the same motion each time you take another signature to pierce holes (see Figure 303).

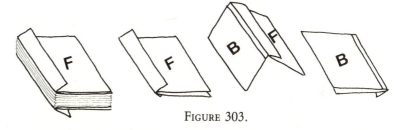

FIGURE 303.

8. Take the flyleaf signature off the stack and insert the piece of bristol so that the fold of the signature fits exactly around the folded bristol. Hold both firmly together and push a needle through the holes in the bristol and the signature folds. This is best done by placing the signature on a board with the fold slightly overhanging so that the needle clears any hard surface. Repeat this step with all signatures (see Figure 304).

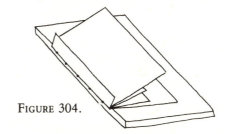

FIGURE 304.

   Note: You may feel more comfortable securing the inner leaves of the signature in place with paper clips.

9. Cut a length of linen thread equal to the height of one signature multiplied by the number of signatures *plus* two extra lengths.

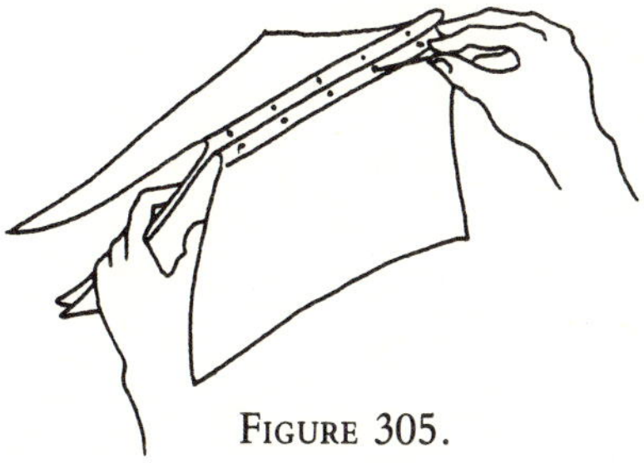

   The signatures are linked by sewing two signatures together at a time (see Figure 305). The sewing on of the second signature is not yet completed when the third signature is added. Stitches go from the third to the second, from the fourth to the third, and so on. Signatures are alternately added at the second and fifth sewing holes. The sewing pattern of the first and last signatures differ slightly from the rest, since each is attached to another signature on one side only (see Figure 306).

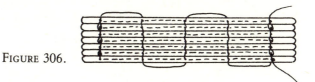

FIGURE 305.

FIGURE 306.

10. Take the top signature from the stack, turn it over, and beginning at the outside, insert the needle through the first hole on your right into the signature. Leave approximately three inches of thread extending. Come out at the second hole (see Figures 307 and 308).

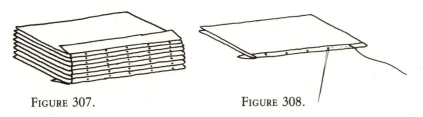

FIGURE 307.   FIGURE 308.

11. Follow the same procedure by taking signature two, turning it over, and placing it on top of signature one. Then insert the needle in through the second hole of signature two and come out at the third hole (see Figure 309).

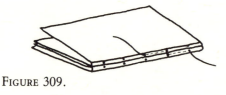

FIGURE 309.

12. Move back to signature one and insert the needle through the third hole and come out at the fourth hole (see Figure 310).

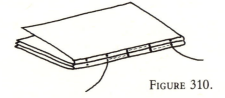

FIGURE 310.

13. Insert the needle in through the fourth hole of signature two and come out at the fifth hole of the same signature (see Figure 311).

FIGURE 311.

14. Insert the needle in through the fifth hole of signature one and come out at the fourth hole of the same signature (see Figure 312).

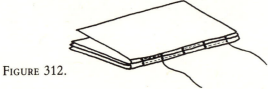

FIGURE 312.

15. Insert the needle in through the third hole of signature one and come out at the second hole of the same signature (see Figure 313).

Figure 313.

16. Gently pull the sewing taut and, with the remaining portion of the sewing thread, tie a square knot (with the three inch tail) as close to the folds as possible (see Figure 314).

Figure 314.

17. Insert the needle through the first hole of signature two and come out of the second hole of the same signature (see Figure 315).

Figure 315.

18. Take signature three from the stack, turn it over, and place it on the two sewn signatures. Go in through the second hole of signature three and come out at the third hole of the same signature (see Figure 316).

Figure 316.

19. Insert the needle in through the third hole of signature two and come out at the fourth hole of the same signature (see Figure 317).

Figure 317.

20. Insert the needle in through the fourth hole of signature three and come out at the fifth hole of the same signature (see Figure 318).

FIGURE 318.

21. Slip the needle between signatures one and two *behind* the connecting thread to form a loop (see Figure 319). Bring the needle through the loop and, pressing the signatures down with your finger, draw the thread tight. This is called a *kettle stitch*, which is made at the two outer sewing holes of each signature to link it to the one below (see Figure 320).

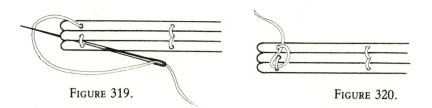

FIGURE 319.   FIGURE 320.

22. Continue in this manner until the last signature is sewn on. The sewing pattern of the *last* signature corresponds with the sewing pattern of the *first* signature. Fasten the thread by making two or three kettle stitches downward. Trim the thread ends to a half an inch.

23. Jog the stack of signatures into alignment and place them between two pressing boards, weighted down with a brick. Using your fingers, apply a thin layer of adhesive to the spine, rub well between the sections, and let the adhesive dry (see Figure 321).

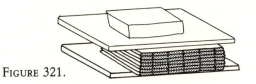

FIGURE 321.

24. Cut a strip of Okawara paper to the height of the signatures by the width of the spine *plus* one and one-half inch. Make creases at the top and bottom of the strip to indicate the middle lengthwise (see Figure 322).

FIGURE 322.

25. Apply a second thin coat of adhesive to the spine, center the Oka-wara paper strip and rub it well with a bone folder through a piece of waste paper (see Figure 323).

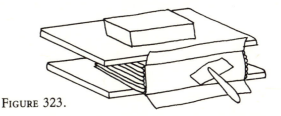

FIGURE 323.

26. After the spine is dry, remove the brick and boards. Brush adhesive on the extending Okawara paper flaps and attach them to the cloth hinges of the flyleaves (see Figure 324).

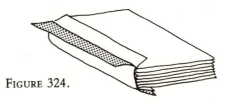

FIGURE 324.

27. Cut a piece of bristol to the height of the signature by four times as wide *plus* the thickness of the spine (see Figure 325).

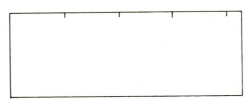

FIGURE 325.

28. Bring the two shorter edges together exactly *without* creasing the strip. Hold them down firmly. Using an awl and a small ruler, pierce two holes. The first hole's distance away from the short edge is equal to the thickness of the spine. Pierce the second hole half an inch in from the first hole (see Figure 326).

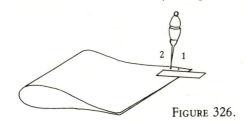

FIGURE 326.

29. Move the top short edge of the bristol back to the first pierced hole (1a) on the bottom portion of the bristol. Make sure that the top and bottom portions of the upper, long edge are aligned. Press the bend down with your thumb, and then crease the bend with a bone folder (see Figure 327).

30. Move the top short edge further back to the second pierced hole (2a) on the bottom portion of the bristol. Press the new bend down with your thumb, crease the bend with the bone folder (see Figure 328).

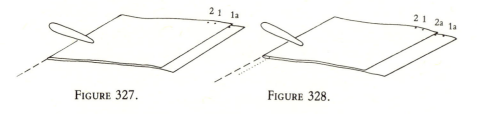

FIGURE 327.   FIGURE 328.

31. Unfold the piece of bristol. Now take the right hand short edge, bring it over to the left and align it with hole number one (see Figure 329). Fold and crease with a bone folder.

32. Move the right hand short edge back to hole number two. Fold and crease (see Figure 330).

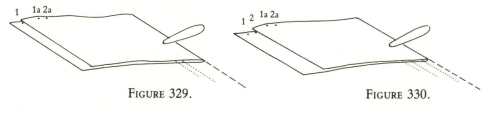

FIGURE 329.   FIGURE 330.

33. Unfold the piece of bristol and reverse the two outer creases (see Figure 331).

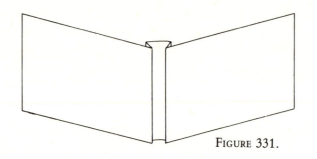

FIGURE 331.

34. Fold the outer short edges to meet the first folds. Using a bone folder, sharpen the fore-edge folds through a piece of waste paper. Fit the bristol around the pamphlet and place it on the table (see Figure 332).

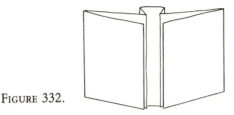

FIGURE 332.

35. Open the front cover and fold the fore-edge flap back. Hold the pamphlet in place with a weight. Slip strips of waxed paper and waste paper underneath the hinge. The waxed paper must be next to the pamphlet and the waste paper next to the hinge. Apply adhesive to the hinge. *Remove and discard the waste paper strips* (see Figure 333).

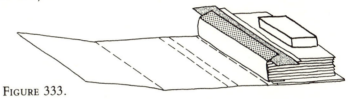

FIGURE 333.

36. Put the weight aside. Hold the pamphlet down firmly with your hand and close the front cover over the adhesive-coated hinge. Using a bone folder, rub down well, through a piece of waste paper (see Figure 334). Place a weight on top and allow the adhesive to dry.

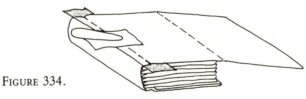

FIGURE 334.

37. Open the cover again. Slip a piece of waste paper underneath the fore-edge flap and apply adhesive (see Figure 335).

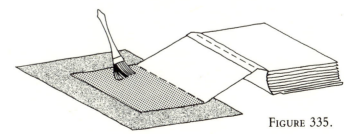

FIGURE 335.

38. Fold and affix the for-edge flap. Insert waxed paper and waste paper. The waxed paper must be next to the pamphlet and the waste paper next to the cover. Close the cover and place a board and weight on top. Let the adhesive dry (see Figure 336).

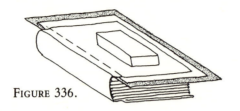

FIGURE 336.

39. Turn the pamphlet over and repeat steps 35–38 for the back cover. Then proceed to step 40.

40. Open and bend back one cover toward the spine. Flatten the bend with a bone folder to sharpen the crease (see Figure 337). Repeat this step on the other side. This process will allow the covers to open easily.

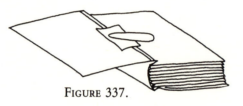

FIGURE 337.

Note: The bristol covers may be reinforced by pasting a strip of book cloth along the spine (see Figure 338) and by inserting pieces of pressboard between the folded bristol of the front and back cover (see Figure 339).

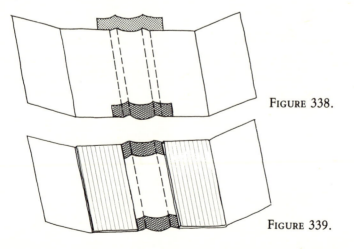

FIGURE 338.

FIGURE 339.

The reinforced bristol covers can also be put on books which do not need to be resewn, but whose covers have fallen off and are too deteriorated to reaffix.

11 | SUPPLY SOURCES

All required materials mentioned in this book may be obtained from one or more of the suppliers listed below. It is a good idea to request a catalog from each supplier to determine what materials each supplies, the minimum quantity that must be ordered and the price and discount structure of each company. Suppliers have been listed based on the knowledge of the staff of their existence, range of available materials, service and economic price structure.

1. Aiko's Art Materials Import
   714 North Wabash Avenue
   Chicago, IL 60611
   (312) 943-0745

2. Basic Crafts Co.
   1201 Broadway
   New York, NY 10001
   (212) 679-3516

3. Bookmakers
   2025 Eye Street, N.W.
   Washington, DC 20006
   (202) 296-6613

4. Conservation Materials, Ltd.
   340 Freeport Boulevard
   Box 2884
   Sparks, NV 89431
   (702) 331-0582

5. Conservation Resources
   International, Inc.
   1111 North Royal St.
   Alexandria, VA 22314
   (703) 549-6610

6. Gane Brothers & Lane, Inc.
   1400 Greenleaf Avenue
   Elk Grove, IL 60007
   (312) 593-3360

7. Gaylord Brothers, Inc.
   Box 4901
   Syracuse, NY 13221
   (315) 457-5070

8. Harcourt Bindery
   9-11 Harcourt Street
   Boston, MA 02116
   (617) 536-5755

9. Hollinger Corporation
   P.O. Box 6185
   Arlington, VA 22206
   (703) 671-6600

10. The Holliston Mills, Inc.
    Box 940
    Hyannis, MA 02601
    (800) 225-7122

11. Joanna Western Mills
    151 West 40 Street
    New York, NY 10018
    (800) 251-7528

12. Light Impressions
    Box 3012
    Rochester, NY 14614
    (800) 828-6216 or
    (716) 271-8960 (in N.Y. State)

13. New York Central Supply Co.
    62 Third Avenue
    New York, NY 10003
    (212) 473-7705

14. Process Materials Corporation
    301 Veterans Boulevard
    Rutherford, NJ 07070
    (201) 935-2900

(Continued on the next page)

(Continued from the previous page)

15. Ernest Schaefer, Inc.
731 Lehigh Avenue
Union, NJ 07083
(201) 964-1280

16. TALAS
130 Fifth Avenue
New York, NY 10011
(212) 675-0718

17. University Products, Inc.
South Canal Street
Box 101
Holyoke, MA 01041
(800) 628-1912

The numbers after each product refer to the list of suppliers above.

Adhesives: see **pp. 44-49 (Chapter 5)**
Book Cloth, Buckram and starch filled: **3, 6, 8, 10, 11, 16**
       Recasing leather: **7**
Bristol: **14, 16, 17**
Cutters and Trimmers: **2, 3, 6, 7, 15, 16, 17**
Envelopes, acid-free: **5, 9, 16, 17**
Japanese Paper: **1, 3, 12, 13, 16, 17**
Lens Tissue, L tissue: **3, 16, 17**
Library Board: **14**
Map Folder Stock: **9**
Opaline* Pad: **13, 16,** or from art supply stores
Pamphlet Binders, ready made: **7, 17**
Paper, Acid-free Bond (e.g. Permalife*): **7, 9, 12, 16, 17**
       Acid-free Tissue: **9, 14, 16, 17**
       Acid-free Wrapping Paper: **12, 14, 16**
       Acid-free Blotting: **12, 14, 16, 17**
       Waxed: **7**
Pressboard: **16, 17**
Presses: **2, 3, 6, 8, 15, 16**
Polyester Film (e.g. Mylar*): **7, 12, 14, 16**
Polyester Web: **16**
Tape, double sided: **7, 12, 16, 17**
Thread, linen: **2, 3, 6, 8, 16, 17**
Tools, hand: see pp. **25-27**

*Reg. T.M.

This annotated bibliography is not intended to be a comprehensive list of books on preservation. It is instead a selective guide that can supplement the information in this manual with works which are currently readily available. The journals included are those that will often provide current information on library materials preservation.

ARTICLES

Avedon, Don M. "Microfilm Permanence and Archival Quality: Standards." *Special Libraries*, 63, 12 (December 1972): 586–88. Reprinted from Journal of Micrographics 6, 2 (November–December 1972).

Standards for microfilm permanence. Archival and other storage conditions are discussed.

Baker, John P., and Marguerite C. Soroka, eds. *Library Conservation Preservation in Perspective*. Stroudsburg, PA, Dawden, Hutchinson & Ross, Inc., 1978.

A selected collection of articles that focuses on *why* materials deteriorate and *why* they must be preserved; *what* should be preserved; *who* should do the work and *how they should do it; and how* individuals from other disciplines must collaborate if conservation is to become a reality.

Banks, Paul N. *The Preservation of Library Materials*. Chicago: The Newberry Library, 1978.

Reprinted from the *Encyclopedia of Library and Information Science*, vol. 23, this pamphlet gives an overview of the preservation field, including problems and some solutions, preservation personnel, research, and standards.

_____. *A Selective Bibliography on the Conservation of Research Library Materials*. Chicago: Newberry Library, 1981.

This selected bibliography provides a wide range of conservation information for both the librarian and the archivist.

Bohem, Hilda. *Disaster Prevention and Disaster Preparedness*. Berkeley: University of California, Systemwide Administration, Library Plans and Policies, 1978.

Gives a concise and clear plan for organizing both a disaster prevention team and a disaster action team within a library, as well as an outline for organizing pre-disaster and disaster operations.

Burdett, Eric. *The Craft of Bookbinding: A Practical Handbook*. New York: Pitman Publishing Corp., 1977.

Essentially material on the craft of hand bookbinding, this book also contains a substantial amount of material on workshop tools, equipment and supplies, protective enclosures, cleaning and repairing techniques. Glossary.

Byrnes, Margaret M. "Preservation of Library Materials: 1981" *Library Resources and Technical Services* 26, 3 (July/Sept 1982): 223–239.

An overview of the state of preservation/conservation through the literature of 1981 shows problems of the 70's beginning to find resolution in the 80's. A follow-up to the Darling/Ogden article in *Library Resources & Technical Services* 25.

Clapp, Anne F. *Curatorial Care of Works of Art on Paper*. Oberlin, Ohio: The Intermuseum Laboratory, 1978.

Although primarily concerned with care of art on paper, much of the information and many of the materials and techniques described are useful in the preservation of library materials. Includes an extensive list of materials, tools, and equipment and their sources.

Cockerell, Sydney M. *Bookbinding and the Care of Books: A Textbook for Bookbinders and Librarians*. London: Pitman Publishing Ltd., 1978.

For bookbinders and librarians, this book is intended to help select sound methods of binding books.

Cunha, George Martin, and Dorothy Grant Cunha, *Conservation of Library Materials, A Manual and Bibliography on the Care, Repair and Restoration of Library Materials*, 2 vols. Metuchen, N.J.: Scarecrow Press, Inc., 1971–72.

Vol. 1 of this two-volume set gives extensive information on the care and preservation of library materials, including the enemies of library materials, preventive care, repair, and disaster information. Various helpful appendices add dimension to the preceding chapters. Vol. II is a comprehensive bibliography in the same format as Vol. 1.

Cunha, George. *What an Institution Can Do to Survey its Conservation Needs*. New York: New York Library Association, Resources & Technical Services Section, 1979.

This publication is a revision of a paper presented in Sept. 1977 at a Conservation Seminar for the NYLA in Syracuse. Through a series of questions, the reader is led through a survey of the library building, its environment and security, the general state of the collection and disaster vulnerability.

Darling, Pamela. "Developing a Preservation Microfilming Program." *Library Journal*, 99 (November 1, 1974): 2803–09.

Discusses library service goals; the nature of collections; the value, uniqueness, and condition of the materials; and the availability of funds that determine microfilming policy and guidelines. Options include buying microforms from a commercial micropublisher or another library, having copy filmed by an outside film agency, or filming in-house.

——————. "Microforms in Libraries: Preservation and Storage," *Microform Review*, 5 (1976): 93–100.

Discusses microforms as a tool for storing and preserving information that traditionally is recorded on paper. Proper methods of storing microforms is covered.

_____. *The Preservation of Library Materials: A CUL Handbook*. New York: Columbia University Libraries, Preservation Department, 1980.

This revised edition of the handbook, first issued in 1976, reflects developments within the Preservation Department of Columbia and the field of preservation/conservation generally. Specific treatment, commercial and in-house, is covered in great detail. Tips on stack maintenance, patron awareness, and how to deal with water disasters are included.

_____ and Sherelyn Ogden. "From problems perceived to programs in practice: the preservation of library resources in the U.S.A., 1956–1980" *Library Resources and Technical Services* 25, 1 (January/March 1981): 9–29.

Major events and activities in the field of preservation/conservation over 25 years and the development of preservation within librarianship. Reference is made to important publications of the period.

Dolloff, Francis W., and Roy Perkinson. *How to Care for Works of Art on Paper*. Boston: Museum of Fine Arts.

Concise information on the properties and care of paper, much of which is applicable to the preservation of library materials.

Frost, Gary. "Conservation Standard Rebinding of Single Books: A Review of Current Practice at the Newberry Library." *AIC Preprints*, 1977, 56–61.

Here are principles and techniques developed for conservation rebinding procedures using a 17th century printed book, poorly rebound in the 19th century, as a prototype.

Greenfield, Jane. *Wraparounds*, Pamphlet 1, New Haven: Yale University Library, 1980.

Detailed, illustrated directions for making a strong preservation enclosure. Includes lists of equipment materials and suppliers, as well as general information on grain of paper, scoring and folding, and other topics.

_____. *Tip-ins and Pockets*, Pamphlet 2. New Haven: Yale University Library, 1980.

Illustrated instructions on the attachment of four different formats: a single leaf, several leaves, a folded sheet, and several folded sheets, one inside another. Equipment, materials, and suppliers are listed. Pockets to be placed inside the back cover for materials that belong with a book are described and illustrated.

_____. *Paper Treatment*, Pamphlet 3. New Haven: Yale University Library, 1981.

Contains techniques suitable for repair of research materials. Treatments explained are cleaning, flattening, some mending, reproduction, provision of handling and storage containers, spray deacidification, and encapsulation. Equipment, materials, and suppliers are listed.

_____. *Pamphlet Binding*, Pamphlet 4. New Haven: Yale University Library, 1981.

Primarily concerned with printed matter less than half an inch thick and bound into a limp cover. Simple hardcover protection is described and illustrated. Equipment, materials, and suppliers are listed.

_____. *The Small Bindery*, Pamphlet 5. New Haven: Yale University Library, 1981.

The equipment and tools needed for making simple repairs are described. Suppliers are listed.

_____. *Hinge & Joint Repair*, Pamphlet 6. New Haven: Yale University Library, 1982.

The most recent in a most helpful series of pamphlets for the librarian and technician responsible for in-house preservation.

Harrison, Alice W. *The Conservation of Library Materials*. Halifax, Nova Scotia: Dalhousie University, 1981.

The author, the first recipient of the Alberta Letts travelling fellowship, reports on over 60 visits to conservation workshops, binderies, museums, libraries, library schools, printers and archives in Canada and seven foreign countries to study methods of preservation and restoration.

Hawken, William R. *Copying Methods Manual*. Chicago: Library Technology Program, American Library Association, 1966.

Covers various processes of reproduction of materials in general, a considerable amount of information on microforms is given with a description and evaluation of each format. In-depth information. Useful illustrations. Glossary.

Horton, Carolyn. *Cleaning and Preserving Bindings and Related Materials*. 2nd Ed. revised. Chicago: American Library Association, LTP Publication No. 16, 1969.

A very practical manual that aids the book preservationist in organizing and carrying out a program of cleaning, repairing, and caring for a variety of library materials. A short glossary is included.

Library of Congress. Photoduplication Service. *Specifications for the Microfilming of Books and Pamphlets in the Library of Congress*. Washington, D.C., 1973. For sale by the Government Printing Office.

This guide clarifies recommended procedures, in use at the Library of Congress, for microfilming monographs.

_____. Photoduplication Service. *Specifications for the Microfilming of Manuscripts in the Library of Congress*. Washington, D.C., 1980. For sale by the Government Printing Office.

Designed as an aid to librarians, this book is also a teaching tool for schools of library science. It outlines commercial binding practices as they are, not necessarily as they should be.

——————————. Photoduplication Service. *Specifications for the Microfilming of Newspapers in the Library of Congress*. Washington, D.C., 1972. For sale by the Government Printing Office.

> This augmented guide further fulfills the function of the earlier edition of 1964 in clarifying procedures. Especially important are the criteria, currently employed at the Library of Congress, for evaluation microfilms under consideration as additions to a permanent collection.

——————————. *Preservation Leaflets*, 1–5. Washington, D.C., 1975.

> This series of leaflets covers a variety of problems prevalent in libraries. No. 1: "Selected References in the Literature of Conservation"; No. 2: "Environmental Protection of Books and Related Materials"; No. 3: "Preserving Leather Bookbindings"; No. 4: "Marking Manuscripts"; No. 5: "Preserving Newspapers and Newspaper-Type Materials."

> Available free of charge from the Library of Congress, Attn: Chief, Preservation Office, Research Services, Washington, D.C. 20540.

——————————. *Polyester Film Encapsulation*. Washington, D.C., 1980.

> Background information on polyester film and its uses for encapsulation, followed by detailed illustrations and directions for making a polyester envelope, are also included. Appendix lists types of polyester film or archival quality and sources of supply.

McCann, Michael. *Artist Beware*. New York: Watson-Guptill, Publications, 1979.

> An extensive work noting the hazards of art and craft materials, which chemicals in what materials are hazardous, how hazardous they are, how they affect the body, and precautions to take when using these materials.

McCrady, Ellen, "Preserving Inner Margins in the Library Bindery," *The Library Scene*, Pt. 1, March 1980, pp. 28–30, and Pt. 2, June 1980, 24–26.

> Pt. one of this two-part series discusses the various sewing methods that preserve inner margins. Pt. two discusses all types of adhesive bindings.

Middleton, Bernard C. *The Restoration of Leather Bindings*. Chicago: American Library Association, LTP Publication No. 18, 1972.

> A detailed explanation that illustrates all phases of leather restoration. Definitions of terms, materials, equipment, and workshop tools are included.

Morrow, Carolyn Clark and Steven B. Schoenly. *A Conservation Bibliography for Librarians, Archivists, and Administrators*. Troy, N.Y.: Whitston Publishing Co., 1979.

> This bibliography cites materials in the field of library conservation which have appeared since 1966. Part I is a selected, classified listing with annotations. Part II is a comprehensive bibliography, in alphabetical order, with citations from Part I repeated. Includes a subject index with "see" references.

_____. *Conservation Treatment Procedures: a manual of step-by-step procedures for the maintenance and repair of library materials.* Littleton, Colorado: Libraries Unlimited, Inc., 1982.

This volume presents a practical approach to hands-on conservation; maintenance, book repair and protective encasement. Added appendices are helpful.

National Conservation Advisory Council *Reports*. Washington, D.C., 1978.

Copies of reports can be ordered from the National Conservation Advisory Council, c/o A&I 2225, Smithsonian Institution, Washington, D.C. 20560. Specific pamphlets are:

_____. *Report of the Study Committee on Education and Training*. Washington, D.C., 1979.

A summary of needs in conservation training and the recommendation of possible ways to satisfy these needs in the future. Appendices include information on existing training programs; however, all are aimed at art conservation.

_____. *Report of the Study Committee on Libraries and Archives: National Needs in Libraries and Archives Conservation.* Washington, D.C., 1980.

A summary of the conservation needs of libraries and archives, this work recommends possibilities for the future aid in fulfilling these needs.

Rabsamen, Werner. "A Study of Simple Binding Methods," a five-part series: *Library Scene*, June, September, December 1979; March, June, 1980.

In this series the characteristics and limits of various binding techniques are discussed. Mechanical and looseleaf binding systems, side-stitching and sewing, overcasting, oversewing, the relatively new cleat laced binding, and adhesive binding are covered. The concluding article discusses covering materials, boards, and adhesives used for covermaking.

Rath, Frederick, L., and Marrilyn Rogers O'Connell, eds. *Care and Conservation of Collections: A Bibliography* vol. 2. Nashville, Tenn., American Association for State and Local History, 1977.

An extensive bibliography on conservation in general, including sections on "Environmental Factors in Conservation," and "Conservation of Library Materials." Entries include monographs, periodicals, and references to specific periodical articles. Some are annotated.

Rice, E. Stevens. *Fiche and Reel*, rev. ed. Ann Arbor, Mich.: Xerox University Microfilms, 1972.

This free booklet answers questions on scholarly micropublishing asked by librarians, educators, scholars, and others who acquire, use, store, exhibit, and explain published microform projects.

Roberts, Matt, T. "The Library Binder." *Library Trends* 24: 749–762, 1976.

Defines library binding. Discusses how a library binder is selected based on a sample of the various available services. An evaluation of the sample lists the principal qualities of good library binding.

Swartzburg, Susan G. *Preserving Library Materials, a Manual.* Metuchen, N.J.: Scarecrow Press, 1980.

Brings up to date much of the materials covered in the two-volume work by G.M. and D.G. Cunha. Includes extensive glossary and bibliography.

Tauber, Maurice F., ed. *Library Binding Manual: A Handbook of Useful Procedures for the Maintenance of Library Volumes.* Boston: Library Binding Institute, 1972.

Designed as an aid to librarians, this book is also a teaching tool for schools of library science. It outlines commercial binding practices as they are, not necessarily as they should be.

Walker, Gay. "Library Binding as a Conservation Measure." *Collection Management* 4: 1/2, 55–71, Spring–Summer 1982.

This article discusses the many choices that librarians, who are responsible for the physical maintenance of important and often unique collections, must make when choosing library binding and repair methods that are the least injurious and that will extend and conserve the life of each volume.

Waters, Peter. *Procedures for Salvage of Water-Damaged Library Materials.* Washington, D.C.: Library of Congress, 1979.

Clear and well-organized information on salvaging water-damaged materials using the freezing method, as well as cleaning and drying with freezing. Appendices give sources of assistance and sources of service, supplies, and equipment.

Young, Laura, S., *Bookbinding and Conservation by Hand.* New York: R.R. Bowker, 1981.

An illustrated handbook of hand bookbinding techniques, conservation repairs and enclosures. A selected bibliography, a list of suppliers, and information on equipment, tools and materials are included.

JOURNALS

The Abbey Newsletter

Covers a variety of topics such as lecture summaries, book reviews, information on conferences, workshops, apprenticeship programs, and equipment for sale, exchange of information, and new supplies and suppliers. Issued six times yearly. Address: *The Abbey Newsletter*, 516 Butler Library, School of Library Service, Columbia University, New York, NY 10027.

Conservation Administration News

Intended for librarians who are responsible for conservation or preservation programs. CAN provides information on preservation efforts in libraries, sources of archival supplies, announcements and reports on conferences and workshops, and so on. Lists reviews and recent publications. Issued quarterly. Address: *Conservation Administration News*, University of Tulsa, McFarlin Library, 600 S. College Ave., Tulsa, OK 74104.

The Library Scene

Published by the Library Binding Institute, this journal includes a wide variety of articles on preservation of library materials, binding techniques and library preservation programs as well as announcements of meetings and workshops. Published bi-annually. Address: *The Library Scene*, P.O. Box 217, Accord, MA 02108.

National Preservation Report

Presents national and international developments in various areas of preservation books, paper, microfilming projects, etc. Published quarterly. Address: *National Preservation Report*, Library of Congress, Washington, D.C. 20540.